15 REASONS

YOUR HOUSE HASN'T SOLD

THE BLUEPRINT TO SELL ANY HOUSE

JOSHUA INGLIS

CONTENTS

FAIL

a Four Letter Word

INTRODUCTION

"Failure isn't fatal, but failure to change might be."
—JOHN WOODEN

FAIL is treated like other bad four-letter words but it is something that happens to each and every person throughout life. If you fail at something, it is nothing to be ashamed of.

Every failure I've had in my life has been a valuable learning experience. You either win or you learn and failure is a necessary teacher to learn, progress, and become better. I believe in failure so much that when I hire someone, one of my interview questions is "tell me of a time when you failed". I don't ask this question to be cruel, I ask this question to find out how my interviewee overcame the failure and what they learned from it.

How does failing apply to real estate? Well you are probably reading this book because you are either a seller or real estate agent that failed to sell a house on the market or you might be thinking of selling your house and want to avoid the same fate as most houses that fail to sell.

You have probably already heard the statistic that 9 out of 10 businesses fail. The good news is that the odds are not that bad when it comes to successfully selling a house. The bad news is that you probably have a better chance of not selling your house when you list it with a real estate agent than you do of actually selling it. It is not a statistic that I could easily find through my research for this book because it is not something that the real estate agent community wants the public to know about. I had to do my own research to find out this information so I looked at different markets. What I found was that the cancelled and expired listings in a year typically outnumbered the sold listings in a 1-year time frame for most markets. I found that in certain markets the cancelled and expired listings (houses that failed to sell) outnumbered the sold listings by over 2.5 to 1! This was not in 2009 after the crash, my research was done in 2016 and 2017 which were both good years for selling real estate.

So who or what is to blame for your house or these houses failing to sell? Is it the markets fault? Not really because houses sell in every market (up, down, or sideways). The market may fluctuate but people will always need a place to live even in the worst markets.

I know what you are probably thinking "It's the real estate agent's fault! They were the ones that didn't do X, Y, and Z!".

That is why in some cases real estate agents have a worse reputation than a used car salesman. Real estate agents have such bad reputations that the Boogey Man checks for real estate agents under his bed before he goes to sleep. All kidding aside, just like any other business or profession there are many bad real estate agents and there are many good real estate agents.

If I called your last real estate agent and asked why the house didn't sell, they might blame you

They might say you were unrealistic with your price, you didn't do the upgrades they requested, you didn't stage the house, you didn't paint, you didn't allow them to do their job properly, etc.

Who is to Blame?

I don't blame you, I don't blame the agent, and I don't blame the market. So who or what is to blame for the house not selling? It is simple, most traditional sales methods are to blame. Insanity can be defined as doing the same thing over and over again expecting different results. That is why it is time to do something different, something drastically different! The only way this book will help is if you implement the sales strategies contained within. There is no magic pill, no easy button, it will take hard work on your part and the real estate agents part. Only then will you be able to sell the house that didn't sell.

Why I'm a Real Estate Agent

I didn't start my real estate career as an agent but as an investor and I purchased my first rental property when I was only 19 years old. I had tenants that were over twice my age and was a landlord. I've made money in real estate through other strategies as well: flipping over 100 properties, building new construction houses as a builder, owning a construction company, collecting rents, wholesaling houses, seller financing houses, having a real estate radio show in Chicago, running the largest real estate meetup that meets in the city of Chicago, being a coach and mentor to aspiring agents and investors across the United States and Canada, public speaking, and being a private money lender (acting like a bank as a mortgagee to a borrower).

Through those experiences I quickly realized that real estate was not about houses, it was about people. Whether it was working with a contractor so they could put food on the table for their family or helping a family purchase a home when they never thought it was possible, real estate is about serving others. Many times in real estate, you are helping someone with one of the biggest decisions they will ever make in their life.

I have been blessed with the opportunity to help and impact thousands of lives in my real estate career thus far and my goal is to help millions. Sometimes it takes just one person to make a difference in someone's life forever and this person impacted me as much as I impacted her. She is the reason why I do what I do which changed my life forever and is the reason why I am a real estate agent today.

When I was just an investor (not a real estate agent at this point), I placed an advertisement in a local phone book directory and I received a call a couple months later from someone who saw my ad and she told me she was looking to sell her house whom I will call Sarah. Sarah told me on the phone that the house needed extensive repairs and I told her that I might be able to help. Sarah was in a very affluent area but the house backed up to a highway.

When I pulled up to the house I could hear the highway but it wasn't as loud as I thought it would be considering it was literally behind the house. I knocked and Sarah came to the door. Sarah was an older lady in her early 60s and was hesitant to let me in due to the condition of the house. I assured her that it was ok and that I had seen worse so she shouldn't worry. She let me in and took me on a tour of the house. The house had a very unique smell that burned your eyes if you were in the house for very long. Sarah had five cats, a rodent problem, and a raccoon problem (I didn't find out about the rodents and raccoons until later). She hadn't vacuumed or cleaned the house in a very long time so there was cat hair and urine everywhere. There was thick carpet from the 80's and the cat hair was intertwined pretty thick. There was a huge blue tarp on the back of the house and it had water leaks in other areas as well. The house was very outdated so almost everything had to be redone.

Sarah appreciated the fact that I did not make a big deal about the condition of the house. She told me that she previously had two real estate agents through the house and they wanted nothing to do with the house unless Sarah fixed the issues with the house and cleaned it out. She did not have the money to fix it up so she was in a really tough spot. She told my brother and I that she almost took a bottle of pills before she met us (to commit suicide) because she felt trapped by the house and there was no way out. The two real estate agents she met with could not help her so I absolutely had to help Sarah, this was a life or death situation. This is when it hit me, I was in the right place at the right time. I felt that I was living my purpose and God had put me there at that moment to save her life.

Sarah was excited that we could help her with the house by purchasing it but was concerned that she did not have anywhere to move. It was hard for her to find a condo within her budget that was in good shape. To address the concern I asked her, "What if I help you find an amazing deal? I'll even help you renovate it." Sarah replied, "That would be fantastic!" We looked at several different properties until she found her perfect condo. The condo she fell in love with was in the same town she currently lived in, was on the first floor which was great so she didn't have to go up any stairs, it backed up to a golf course, and her son previously worked at a restaurant across the street. She knew that this was the one!

I purchased the condo before she sold us the house. We did a renovation to the condo before she moved in where we put in a new kitchen, painted it, installed tile, and did remodeling in both bathrooms. She absolutely loved her new place and moved into the renovated condo on the day that we purchased her house and paid off the mortgage on her old house. She did not have to bring a dime to closing and we gave her title to the condo so that she owned the condo free and clear with no mortgage.

Sarah is still a very good friend of mine and I am glad we were able to help her through this difficult time and that we reached her when we did. Sarah loves her condo and no longer has the debt and burden of a house she couldn't afford. I smile when I reflect on stories like this one knowing that we changed someone's life for the better and is proof that **this business saves lives**.

I had an epiphany through all of this, if I was a real estate agent I might have been one of the two real estate agents that she met with originally and been able to help her before she got to the point of near suicide. I realized to do the most good, I needed to become a licensed real estate agent. After all, I've purchased and sold more of my own properties than many agents have sold for other people. Since then, I have sold her former neighbor's house as a real estate agent and several other houses in her neighborhood.

Her next door neighbor was in a very similar situation and called me because she knew what I did for Sarah. It was a situation where Tammy (the neighbor) had the house listed with a previous agent but was unable to sell because of the houses condition and poor marketing. In this situation, Tammy's best option was to fix up the house and list it so it was good that I became licensed after working with Sarah. Tammy owned a condo in Florida and could not afford to make the payments on the house anymore while owning the condo. The stress of it all even put her in the hospital for a couple of days. I helped her renovate the house with my contractors in order to get it sold and we even fronted the money for the work to get done since she did not have any money to do the work herself. If I had not been a licensed agent, Tammy could have been in a very similar situation to Sarah, stuck with no options and trapped by the house. Tammy, Sarah, and many of the other families I have helped are the reason I do what I do. It is my goal to impact millions of lives and create a ripple effect in their lives that will impact their family, their friends, their co-workers, their acquaintances, and grandchildren.

I did not write this book to bash other real estate agents, it is just most real estate agents have a box and only know how to operate within that box, I want to encourage out of the box thinking so as a community we can do better!

The Solution

So now that you know a little bit about me, my background, and why I do this, lets focus on YOU! Let's get into the meat and potatoes of why your house hasn't sold. There are 15 possible reasons why your house hasn't sold and there are 15 chapters so let's roll up our sleeves and get to work.

Note: I will be using the word house throughout the entire book. This book applies whether you have a house, a condo, a business, or a commercial piece of property. Also, I wrote this book as if you tried selling your house once before and were unsuccessful. The principles in this book apply whether you tried selling your house in the past or if you want to list your house for the very first time.

YOUR HOUSE IS UNDERPRICED

CHAPTER 1

"Marketing without data is like driving with your eyes closed." —DAN ZARELLA

Most agents will underprice a house or price a house that results in less exposure because of how buyers are searching online. Most agents will incorrectly price a house by $1, $100, or $1000. How many times do you see a million dollar house listed for $999,999 , $999,900, or $999,000? The answer is almost every time. This is the biggest mistake that most real estate agents make.

Many agents list at those prices for the same reason that candy bars are 99 cents. 99 cents sounds cheaper than one dollar. The problem with this logic is that buyers online look at price ranges in $10,000, $25,000, & $50,000 increments, not $1,000 increments. For example, if a buyer's pre-approval letter is for $1,200,000, they are probably set up on a search to look at houses priced between $1,000,000 - $1,250,000. They are most likely not set up on a price range search to look at houses between $999,000-$1,249,000 and now the house is not even seen by those buyers when the house is listed at $999,000.

When my team and I list a house, we run a detailed comparative market analysis and use reverse prospecting for market research to price the house for optimum exposure.

What is reverse prospecting you ask? Reverse prospecting is a tool that allows us to see how many buyers working with agents are looking at houses at various price points utilizing the MLS. We can see exactly how many buyers working with agents are looking for a house with your house's features at $499,000. We can also see how many buyers are looking at $500,000 and how many buyers are looking for a property with your house's features at any price point.

Let's run a very basic example of a listing where houses are selling between 190k and 200k. We run multiple scenarios and incorporate the property's features to strategically price the house.

What do you think the list price should be? Should you list the house at $210,000 so that way you can negotiate down? Should you be conservative and list the house at $190,000? Should you try to trick the buyer into thinking they are getting a better deal by listing it at $199,000. Or should you list the house at $200,000? Let's look at the data from reverse prospecting and find out with a real example.

Here are the results:

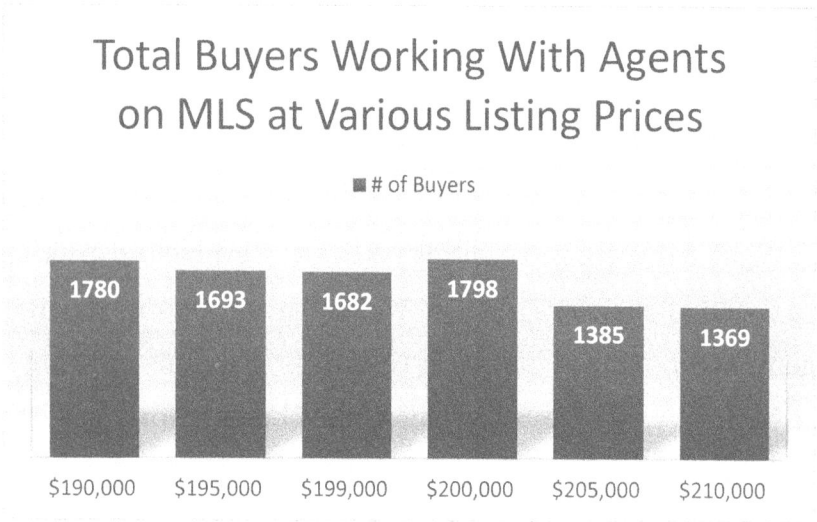

Total Buyers Working With Agents on MLS at Various Listing Prices

■ # of Buyers

$190,000	$195,000	$199,000	$200,000	$205,000	$210,000
1780	1693	1682	1798	1385	1369

$190,000 – 1,780 buyers set up on automatic MLS searches

$195,000 – 1,693 buyers set up on automatic MLS searches

$199,000 – 1,682 buyers set up on automatic MLS searches

$200,000 – 1,798 buyers set up on automatic MLS searches

$205,000 – 1,385 buyers set up on automatic MLS searches

$210,000 – 1,369 buyers set up on automatic MLS searches

As you can see, there are the most buyers at $200,000! There are actually fewer buyers at $190,000 even by pricing the house $10,000 cheaper! That's how underpricing your house can hurt the exposure if you do not look at the data. What's even more surprising is that there are 116 fewer buyers searching at $199,000 than $200,000! Always look at the numbers because it only takes one person to buy a house.

There is a very good chance that the house is a good fit for at least one or two of those 116 buyers.

A house listed at $199,000 may have 2-8% fewer buyers than a house that is listed at $200,000 in a neighborhood. If an agent ever suggests an odd number like $199,000, $199,274, $399,000, 449,000, or $999,990 they have not looked at the data because there are always fewer buyers on odd numbers.

The data mentioned above are for buyers working with an agent utilizing the MLS. This number is astronomically higher when third party sites like Zillow, Trulia, etc. are accounted for. Most buyers start their house search online on their own before they ever contact a real estate agent. To prove this point further, take some time and look at how all the consumer websites are set up and see if my explanation lines up. Very few third-party sites have an option to look at houses starting at $499,000. If you listed a half million-dollar house at $499,000, your house would not be seen by buyers on Zillow, Trulia, Redfin, Realtor.com and thousands of other sites for buyers looking at houses $500,000 and higher.

Don't believe me? Jump on a third-party site or look at the examples on the next two pages.

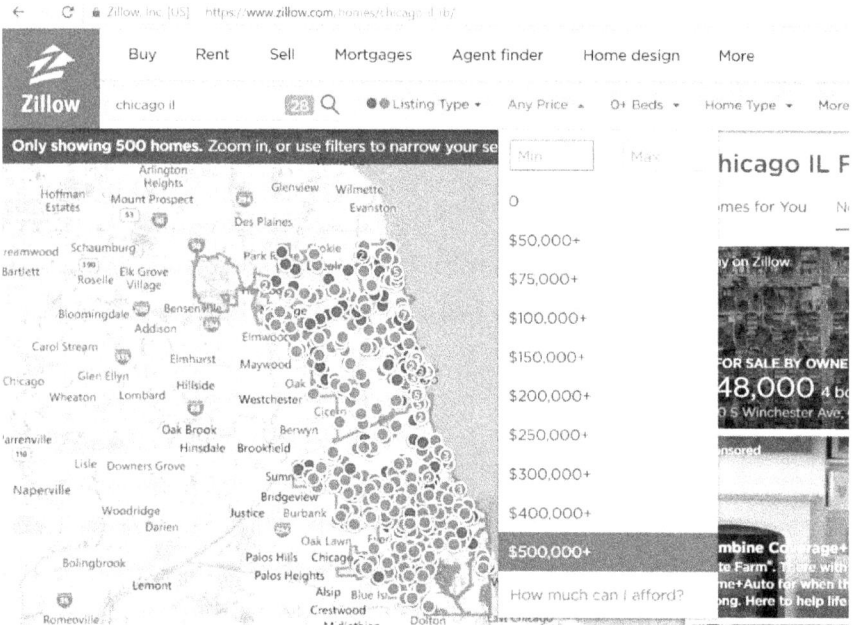

Pictured above: Zillow - minimum price selection $500,000+

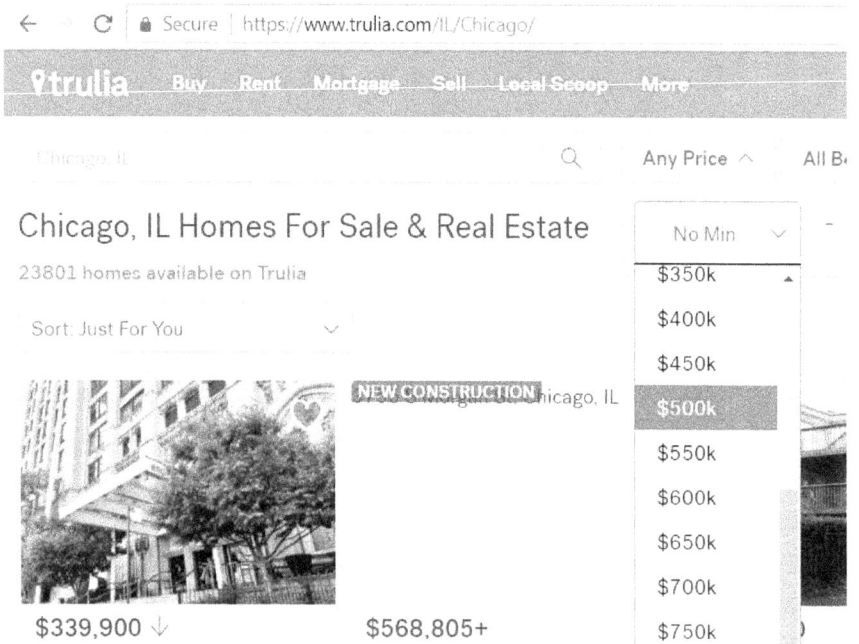

Pictured above: Trulia - minimum price selection $500k

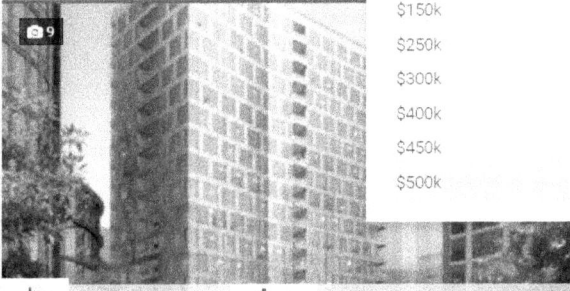

Pictured above: Realtor.com - minimum price selection $500k

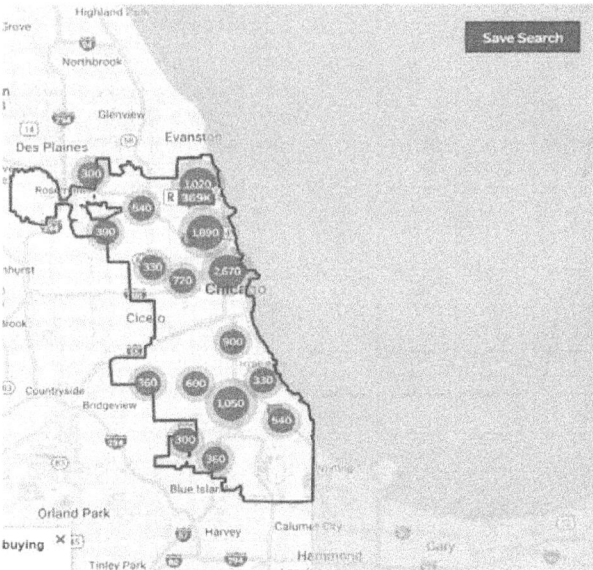

Pictured above: Redfin - minimum price selection $500k

In Summary

If an agent ever tells you to list your house at $xx9,xxx, make sure to educate them on why this is a BIG mistake that can cost YOU thousands of dollars and give you less exposure. If you take away anything from reading this book, know how to price your house strategically using an even number. Make sure the agent you hire uses reverse prospecting for market research to give your house maximum exposure to the market place so you can sell your house for the highest amount possible in the shortest amount of time.

Now that your house has maximum exposure and can be found by buyers, how do you grab buyers' attention and make your house stand out?

YOUR HOUSE DOESN'T
STAND OUT
CHAPTER 2

"Be the one to stand out in a crowd." —JOEL OSTEEN

Professional high-resolution photos are as necessary as the air you are breathing right now when selling your house. You cannot grab potential buyers' attention with lackluster photos.

It all starts with a photo as the foundation for your success in selling. If your house does not have the most vibrant and high-resolution photos, your house will not get the attention it deserves and will be over looked. Buyers make a split decision subconsciously whether they are interested in a house or not when they see it on a real estate website. Buyers can look at 10 listings in under a minute with the power of technology. If your house does not stand out with stunning photos, potential buyers will overlook your house. If the buyer clicks next or not interested, they will likely never see your house again. Professional photography should be real estate 101 but many houses for sale do not have professional photos and professional editing done to them.

FRONT PHOTO

The most important photo is the front photo. The front photo must catch a buyer's eye so they want to see more. That is why you want the first photo to be perfect. Here are some tips to make the first photo pop.

Landscape Bushes/ Remove Trees

If you have a tree or bush that hides part of the house, get rid of it or trim it. You do not want bushes or trees that go above any windows. It is best to plant small shrubs and flowers so the house is showcased. The grass should be mowed, the landscaping should look nice, and there should not be any trash or debris in the yard. If there is a big tree blocking the view for the front of the house, you will want to remove it. You want the house to have as much curb appeal as possible.

On the next page is an example of a house that was marketed over the course of 681 days between two different agents that were both unable to sell it. When I saw the house online, I immediately knew what the problem was. The house had a beautiful peak in the roof line and it was blocked by a large tree. We removed the large tree to give the house curb appeal and we sold the house in 92 days.

Pictured above: Previous photo with large tree in the front.

Pictured above: Our photo after removing the tree

Paint Siding for Curb Appeal

If you have aluminum or wood siding, painting is an inexpensive alternative to replacing the current siding. It is amazing what a fresh coat of paint can do to drastically change the look of the house. Even a garage door can be painted and make a huge difference for your curb appeal.

Sealcoat Driveway/Clean Driveway

If the driveway is asphalt and is level you should sealcoat the driveway before listing the property. If the asphalt driveway is fading, it looks bad and puts a bad seed in some buyers' minds that the driveway will have to be replaced even if it doesn't. Sealcoating a driveway is very inexpensive and will make the house much more appealing. If the driveway is currently concrete and has oil spots and/or stains, a thorough cleaning job should be done.

Timing is Everything

It is ideal to take the photo when the sun is shining on the front of the house, so let the photographer know when the sun hits the front of the house to get the best shot. Between 11am – 2pm is always a safe time to get photos since the sun is usually at its highest peak. The photographer can get photos of the inside if the sun isn't at the front of the house when they first get there. By the time they are done with the inside, the sun will likely be shining on the front of the house.

If you cannot get photos on a bright sunny day, the real estate agent can pay for photoshopping to make the sky blue and the grass green. If the front photo looks dreary or depressing, it will not appeal to buyers and they may not look at any of your other photos because they hit next or not interested online.

Drone & Aerial Photos

Most photographs of houses for sale are virtually identical in terms of how they are shot. There are photos of the outside from ground level and inside from floor level that provide a good, but not great presentation of the house itself. That is why drone shots and video are a wonderful form of promotion that highlight the neighborhood, lot, and views of the house. If the house sits on a large parcel of land, the drone should get a photo that shows the entire lot. If the house has a city or water view, the drone photo can show the subject house and the beautiful view in the same photo. I believe in aerial photography and video so much that I own two drones.

At a minimum, the photographer should have a ladder so that they can get high shots of the house and give another perspective and unique angle.

Twilight Photos

It is always nice to have twilight pictures for your house. It will help your house stand out from the competition of other houses for sale. You want to take the picture right as the sun is going down and have all the lights on in the house and outside. You can get a very unique and beautiful photo during twilight. In many cases, I will make my first photo of the house a twilight photo on the internet and marketing, it makes the house stand out from all the other houses for sale in the area. Twilight photos will draw buyer's attention to your house compared to the other hundreds or thousands of houses online. Twilight photos are also very good to use if your house does not have much curb appeal.

Pictured above: Twilight photo for one of my listings.

Interior Photos

You will want to get as many good interior photos as possible. The professional photographer should take more than 25 photos if you have a large house and it is decorated and staged well. I have listed houses where we used over 80 photos in the marketing. I want to keep buyers going through all the photos and spend as much time as possible looking at your house.

I want to make sure that the photographer takes photos for all of the special features that the house has. If the closets have custom built closet organizers, I want photos of those organizers because buyers love storage and organization. If the house has a beautiful curved staircase, I want to capture that in a few of the photos. All of the house's unique features that can be captured by photos, we take. We do this because we want buyers to schedule a showing that appreciate all the special features that your house has.

The photographer must use a wide-angle lens for all interior photos. A wide-angle lens captures more of the room and makes the rooms look bigger. If you do not use a wide-angle lens for your photos and there is another listing in your neighborhood that does, buyers will think the other house is bigger than your house even if the houses are identical in size. Perception is reality when it comes to photography. We want to trigger the part of the buyer's brain that says: "Yes, I am interested!"

All of the interior photos must be full of light and bright. I see dark photos taken inside of sellers' houses on my local MLS every day which makes my job easier because that is my competition. The saddest part of it is the MLS has a brighten feature built right into it. It would take an agent 3 seconds to brighten a photo and yet agents do not take the time to do it in many cases!

In Summary

Hiring a professional photographer is a must whether you hire an agent or you try to list the house yourself. The photos must be high resolution, bright, and taken with a wide-angle lens. If your agent does not invest in the best photos possible, your house is going to be overlooked by potential buyers.

Are professional photos enough to stand out from the competition?

YOUR HOUSE HAS A
BORING SLIDESHOW
CHAPTER 3

"The only rule is don't be boring & dress cute wherever you go. Life is too short to blend in." —PARIS HILTON

Professional photos are just not enough to help you stand out from the competition. A highly upgraded virtual tour is necessary to help you stand out from other houses for sale. What is a virtual tour? A virtual tour is media that brings your house to life with images, video, and music.

Some people are visual, some people are auditory, and some people are kinesthetic which is why it is important to have different kinds of virtual tours. I am going to break down the different virtual tours that are available and which ones your agent should be doing.

Pictures and Music Slideshow:

I hear real estate agents that brag they use virtual tours on their listings. What they call a virtual tour is pictures with music. That is not a virtual tour! It's a cheap slide show with elevator music. It takes very little effort and costs nothing to do. 90% or more of the virtual tours on the MLS today are exactly this. Unless your house value is less than $100,000, your real estate agent should be investing in something better than a slideshow with music. The pictures and music slideshow should only be supplementary to the other types of virtual tours.

Professionally Narrated Virtual Tour

This is a big step up and an upgrade from the pictures and music slideshow. A professional script writer is hired to create a story about your house and highlights the features of your house. A voice actor is then hired to narrate the pictures while the slideshow plays with music.

This can be effective because the script is written in a way to make the person watching the video feel at home. It also allows the viewer to learn things about the house that they cannot by looking at pictures and music. For example, the voice actor will talk about the school district, the location of the house, and may talk about high-end brands like Rohl water fixtures, Wolf appliances, or other items.

This appeals to buyers who are visual and auditory. A professionally narrated virtual tour is used by very few agents out there because of the cost for hiring a script writer and narrator.

High Definition Video Virtual Tour

This is an even bigger step up from the pictures and music slideshow. High quality video is shot of your house by a professional videographer. This is great because it simulates how buyers would walk through the house and feels much more natural than a picture zooming in and out or a picture panning left to right. There is a big difference between a picture slideshow and actual video of your house in high definition.

High definition video is something that your agent needs to hire a professional to do. There are equipment and strategies to filming video so high-quality scenes are produced. The videographer should have stabilizers and sliders which make the video shots smooth so buyers do not get motion sickness when watching the video. Having faucets on in the bathrooms and kitchen is a technique we use to show buyers it is live video.

With the high definition video virtual tour, it allows the real estate agent to personally invite buyers into the house which gives your house a personal connection. The real estate agent can share their favorite features about the house and can even share a story you want them to tell. This appeals to buyers who are visual and auditory. The high definition video virtual tour is used by very few agents out there because of the cost associated with producing it. Most real estate agents are cheap and try to maximize their comissions so investing in high definition video is scary to them, especially if they are not confident they can sell your house.

Pictured above: Sharing some of my favorite features about my listing on video.

For an example of high definition video virtual tours visit www.joshuainglis.com/highdefvideos

Video Virtual Tour with Actors

Buyers love to buy but hate being sold. That is why many commercials on tv sell a dream or lifestyle that can be achieved by using a product or service compared to having a tv commercial that just lists all the features and benefits that the product offers. Commercials that just list features and benefits would be extremely boring and people would change the channel. If a soda company did a commercial only listing the features and benefits of drinking soda they would go out of business because they would show how much sugar is in the soda, how it rots your teeth, how it causes obesity, how a can is made of aluminum, etc. That is why the commercials for the Superbowl have very little to do with the sponsor of the commercial. The advertisers try to make the audience laugh or make an impact so people talk about the commercial at work the following day.

That is why a virtual tour with actors is powerful. It is a way to sell the house without selling it. It is a unique and fun way to get your house in front of more buyers where people will share the content that is created for the house.

In order to create the high production video, I hire a producer, script writer, film crew, and actors. The producer and script writer then work together to make my idea or outline into a commercial about the house.

Below are some ideas for virtual tours which are a way to sell the house without selling:

One commercial might be where a husband is preparing a romantic dinner for his wife. While he is making dinner in the gourmet kitchen, the wife is getting ready in the master bathroom suite. This video highlights the two things that typically sell houses, kitchens and bathrooms. They might then eat dinner in the formal dining room and dance on the roof top deck under the stars.

Another commercial might be where someone is coming home from the office and a voice actor describes features of the house while the person walks through the house. The video might show the person going into the finished basement to watch a movie in the entertainment room, go for a swim in the pool, go onto the deck to enjoy the views, get a bite to eat in the kitchen, etc. It might also show the person going for a run in the neighborhood to showcase the area. The beauty of this video is that it highlights the lifestyle that the potential buyer can achieve if they purchase the house.

One of my favorite commercials we have done is where a group of kids play hide and seek in the house. The kids are scripted to talk about the features of the house and showcase the important rooms like the kitchen and master bathroom. This is especially effective for large houses.

The sky is the limit with a little creativity. What is great about this form of promotion is that buyers will watch the video because it is unlike any other virtual tour they have ever seen before. It is a way to showcase the house with a story and people love to watch interesting stories.

Pictured above: Shooting a video virtual tour with actors on my listing

Pictured above: Shooting a video virtual tour with child actors on my listing

In Summary

Unless your house is listed for less than $100,000, the agent you hire should be using a professionally narrated tour or a high definition video virtual tour if you want to sell your house. The high definition video virtual tour is preferred which I use on my listings whether it's a small studio condo or a ten thousand square foot estate. If you have a luxury house, your agent should be doing a high definition video and a video virtual tour with actors. Your house is probably the largest investment you own and you are entering a competition with hundreds to thousands of houses for sale. If you don't find a way to stand out, your house will be overlooked online or forgotten. You want your house to be unforgettable in the buyers' minds!

Now that your house is appealing to visual and auditory buyers, how do you appeal to the buyers that are kinesthetic?

BUYERS DON'T KNOW
YOUR LAYOUT
CHAPTER 4

"A confused mind always says no." —UNKNOWN

Kinesthetic buyers like to interact with your house online which is why we include floor plans and a 3D tour. This allows buyers to engage with the home and learn the flow and floor plan before they ever step foot in your house.

We also want to make sure that all buyers that come to see the house are a good fit for it if you are still living at the house to eliminate unnecessary showings. This way you do not waste your time on showings for people that are not serious.

Floor Plans

Floor plans are a great way for potential buyers to get the lay of the land and room dimensions. If a buyer is looking for a house with a 16' by 16' minimum master bedroom for their California king and oversized dressers, you do not want to waste your time showing them your house if your master bedroom is only 12' by 13'. Another example is a buyer who is looking for a first-floor full bathroom and a bedroom or office that can be converted into a bedroom. Why waste your time by showing them your house if they are looking for very specific features that your house does not have.

The showing process can be very lengthy. The time it takes to pack up the kids, pick up the dog, clean up the house, make the house presentable, and go somewhere for an hour can take 2-4 hours. This is very inconvenient for a potential seller and is a very stressful and tedious process for the entire family. If you are still living in the house you are trying to sell, the real estate agent should invest in floor plans so that some of the unnecessary showings can be eliminated.

I'll give you an example of how floor plans can also help sell houses and not just eliminate unnecessary showings. I had a buyer contact me specifically because the house had a first-floor bedroom (a room does not need a closet to be considered a bedroom), a first-floor full bathroom, and a first-floor laundry. He said the house was perfect because he needed a place for his elderly mother on the first floor to stay and she loved doing laundry. We purposely called it a bedroom even though the previous agent called it an office. So why did we call it a bedroom when the previous agent didn't and why did we specify it as a bedroom on the floor plans? The biggest reason for this was because there was a full bathroom next to the room. In this area, many buyers have their elderly mom or dad live with them. Having stairs to go up for an elderly person is a challenge so having a first-floor bedroom and full bathroom is necessary for this kind of living arrangement. This room did not have a closet but had an enormous closet on the other side of the wall that could easily be converted into a large walk in closet for the room. Had they not seen the floor plans, this buyer would have never contacted me. Below is a picture of the floor plans zoomed in to see the bedroom, bathroom, laundry room, and closet that could be easily flipped.

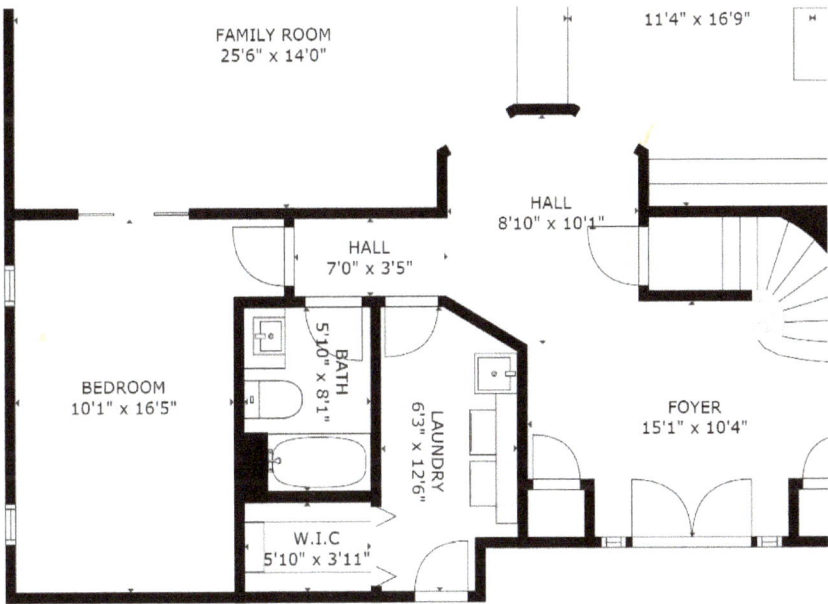

Pictured above: Floorplans from one of my listings

3D Virtual Tour

Have you ever seen pictures of a house online and then are stunned when you walk into the house because it is completely different than what you imagined? Either the flow of the house is different or the layout is different than what you expected. 3D virtual tours are changing that and it is the wave of the future!

3D virtual tours are for the visual and kinesthetic buyer because it allows buyers to virtually walk through your entire house room by room and the buyer feels like they are already inside the house. The buyer can virtually walk around the house at their own leisure. All they need to do is click or touch where they want to walk and they can go there.

What is great about this technology is that it allows buyers from other states or even other countries to see your home's layout and feel. Buyers can now confidently make an offer without ever physically stepping in your house. That is pretty awesome! When a 3D virtual tour is created, it creates a digital floor plan for your house as well.

Buyers can access the 3D tour from a smart phone, tablet, computer, or virtual reality headset. They can look left, right, up, and down in 360 degrees at various points throughout the house like they are there in person.

No matter how good photos are, a person can never really tell how a house feels and what the true layout is. I have shown houses countless times where a buyer will tell me, "This isn't what I thought the house was like" or "I don't like the layout." If the house has a 3D tour, it will help eliminate unnecessary showings for sellers because the people looking can virtually walk themselves through a house and take as much time as they like.

The biggest benefit to the 3D tour is the amount of time that buyers spend using it. I have seen where potential buyers have spent over an hour looking at the house virtually through the 3D tour. This gets buyers to slow down and focus on your house instead of clicking though other listings on the internet.

3D tours also eliminate multiple showings before a buyer takes action. I sold a $1,000,000 listing in a single day because of the power of the 3D tour where the previous agent failed to sell the house. Commonly on a million-dollar listing, the potential buyer will have to see a house 2-5 times before they pull the trigger and take action. This was not the case for this house because I only had to show these buyers the house once before getting the offer. The buyers were confident in making the offer because they utilized the 3D tour and virtually walked through the house several times after the initial showing.

I have also been able to get buyers to make an offer without one of the spouses seeing the house in person, which is not typical. I'll give you an example of a house I sold with this exact scenario, the husband was on a business trip so he was unable to see the house and it was a time sensitive situation. I gave them the link to the 3D tour so the husband could confidently give his blessing on purchasing the house even though he never physically stepped foot in the house. The husband walked through the house virtually with the 3D tour and agreed with his wife that he loved the house too so they made an offer.

Let's use another example because there are many overseas investors purchasing houses in the United States. If a foreign investor living in another country wants to make an offer on a house without coming to the local market where the house is located, which house do you think they would be more confident purchasing:

1. A house with only pictures
2. A house with high definition pictures, aerial photography, high resolution video, floor plans, and a 3d tour so they can virtually walk through the house

The answer is obviously 2, the more information you give a potential buyer (overseas or local), the more confidence that buyer will have in their purchase which translates to more money for the seller. On the flip side, the less consumer confidence a buyer has, the less a buyer will offer (if they make an offer).

Keep in mind there are some downsides to using this 3D technology if your house needs work done to it because it allows buyers to look at every nook and cranny of your house. I have had buyers mention to me about holes in doors or bad paint jobs on trim that I wasn't even aware of because they spent the time to go through the house room by room and look at all the minor details of the house.

For an example of a 3D virtual tour visit any of my 3d tour websites. Some of my 3D tour websites are www.house3dtour.com , www.home3dtour.com , www.chicago3dtour.com , www.condo3dtour.com , and www.3dtourluxury.com

In Summary

Floor plans and 3D tours are great for kinesthetic buyers because it allows them to interact with your house online and spend time virtually walking through your house. Having floor plans and a 3D tour will help to eliminate unnecessary showings and increase qualified showings. It allows buyers to make offers quickly and more confidently without the buyer having to schedule multiple showings to come to a decision. It also allows decision makers to confidently give their ok even if they don't make it to a physical showing inside the house.

So now that buyers know your floor plan, layout, and have virtually walked through the house with a 3D tour, where do they put the furniture?

YOUR HOUSE IS NOT

STAGED

CHAPTER 5

"The investment of staging in your home is far less than a price reduction on your home." —BARB SCHWARZ

If your house is completely empty without furniture, it will probably be difficult to sell. Photos of empty rooms like the living room do not look good, even with the best photographer and highest picture quality. There is no megapixel setting on a camera that will make a photo of an empty room with carpet look stunning. Pictures of empty houses are typically associated with foreclosures, motivated sellers, or houses that need work. Obviously, this is not always the case and you want to present your house in the best manner possible.

If your house has any empty rooms, is vacant, or has outdated furniture, you may want to consider staging the house. So what is staging? Staging is the act of decorating a house to make it appealing. The goal of staging is to make a property appeal to the most buyers which then helps sell a house quickly for top dollar. Staging can be done with furniture, towels, rugs, paintings, curtains, tables, bar stools, chairs, etc.

I know investors that purchase foreclosed and distressed houses and flip them doing very little work. All they do is clean the house, replace carpets, paint, and stage the house with nice furniture. They increase the value of the house by 20-40% by doing these small things! The very nice and expensive furniture that they use to stage the house makes the house feel more luxurious and expensive.

Beware of Bad Staging

I have seen houses that were "staged" and it did not help sell the house, it actually hindered the ability to sell it. I have seen cheap looking furniture used as staging in luxury homes and furniture that does not go with the rest of the décor in the house. There are houses that are "staged" where they used very modern furniture for a very traditional house and vice versa. There are also "staged" houses where they use conflicting color schemes with the staging which ruined the appeal of a room instead of complimentary colors. Be careful to mix color combinations in a room without understanding them.

Just like photography, a professional stager should be used or consulted before any actual staging takes place. That is why I will have my professional stager consult with my seller for many listings. The professional stager will give ideas on what to do and what not to do.

Remember: The goal is not to appeal to your personal taste or liking, but to appeal to as many potential buyers as possible.

Light Staging

Light staging should be used on a house that is listed and vacant. This can be as simple as having a towel with a rope around it in the bathroom. You can add a painting or a small fake plant as well. See photo below for example.

Pictured above: Photo from one of my listings with bathroom lightly staged

Some light-staging ideas for the kitchen are stools for the island with place mats, fancy dinner ware, a cook book, fancy oils or wine, and a flower centerpiece on the island. See photo below for example.

Pictured above: Photo from one of my listings with kitchen lightly staged

In the master bedroom or living room, luxurious looking curtains can be added (especially if you have dated wood trim). You can also add paintings, rugs, or small furniture. Remember that even light-staging can be done incorrectly so it is best to consult with a professional.

A very easy way to lightly stage a house is with a piece of paper most people have in a filing cabinet somewhere. If a house is in a coveted school district, I have my clients put a diploma from a school on the desk in one of the bedrooms so potential buyers will see the diploma immediately when they walk into the room. I will also have my sellers hang a letterman jacket from the school over the chair to the desk in case the buyer does not see the diploma. This will reiterate to a buyer why your house is more desirable than the houses they saw across town with more square footage but in a less coveted school district. Many buyers will sacrifice bedrooms, bathrooms, square footage, a finished basement, or high-end finishes because their children's future is more important than the houses physical features and benefits. That is why you want to reiterate the school with staging if your house features the better schools in the area.

Note: Do not advertise the schools or district with staging if you are in the less desirable ones for the area or it will backfire.

Full Staging

To physically stage a house professionally, it typically costs anywhere between $3,500 - $15,000 for 3 months depending on the size of the house. This is the preferred way to stage a house but is a sizeable investment.

Professional staging makes the photos, the video, and the 3D tour for the house look spectacular. When potential buyers physically see the house, it helps them visualize how to place their furniture and helps them feel at home with decorating ideas.

Sometimes it is hard to justify spending the money for staging but not when you take into consideration the return you get. According to the National Association of Realtors, for every $100 invested in staging, the potential return is $400.

If your house has an unusual or awkward floor plan you must invest in full physical staging to sell your house for top dollar. A professional stager can make even the worst layouts for a house appealing with strategic furniture placement. The reason I say this is necessary for houses with unusual or awkward floor plans is because buyers will not be able to figure out where to place furniture or how-to layout a room. You never want to confuse a potential buyer, you want to give a potential buyer the warm-and-fuzzy feeling about the house. Staging the house will show the buyer that every room is functional and will not leave them questioning the house. If you live in the Chicagoland area and are reading this book I am more than happy to recommend my stagers to you whether you work with me or not.

Virtual Staging

Not convinced to spend the money on staging? Well I have good news for you! The real estate agent should foot the bill to stage the house...virtually!

That's right! Virtually! My listings are staged virtually if there are empty rooms.

Why do I stage my listings virtually? Many buyers cannot visualize an open space like a living room or family room. When I show vacant houses to families, the husband and wife will ask each other "Where are we going to put the couch?" Virtual staging gives them a very good idea for furniture placement and how the house looks before and after virtual staging.

When my brother tried to sell his townhouse, he attempted to do so while he lived there for a couple weeks. He had very few showings because his house did not photograph well because his family outgrew the house and it felt cramped in pictures and in person. It was hard to move things into storage with the baby and one on the way. Once he moved out of the house, he also moved all of the furniture out of the house. I virtually staged the house and relisted at the same exact list price. We had multiple offers and sold over the asking price.

As an example of how virtual staging works similar to regular full staging, I sold a completely vacant empty house in a neighborhood which was the highest sales price in over 9 years (63 other houses sold in that time)! We sold our house for more than the fully renovated houses and the houses that were staged physically. Everyone was attracted to the house because of how good the photos looked virtually staged. The photos would have been bland if we did not virtually stage and we probably would not have sold for as much as we did.

The technology for virtual staging has become so good that most buyers think the staging is real. When I virtually stage a house, most buyers ask me, "Where did all the furniture go?", "Did the owners just move out?", I then explain that the furniture is not real and it is digital. Here are some photo examples of listings I have virtually staged.

JOSHUA INGLIS

JOSHUA INGLIS

In Summary

Staging is a must if you want to sell your house quickly and for top dollar. Photos always look better when they are staged physically or virtually. If you do not want to spend the money to stage the house, the real estate agent should invest to virtually stage the empty rooms in the house. Not staging a house either physically or virtually can cost you tens of thousands of dollars since the house is not presented in the best manner possible.

Now that your house is professionally staged and looks great in photos, what about your web presence?

YOUR HOUSE DOESN'T HAVE
A WEBSITE
CHAPTER 6

"Websites promote you 24/7: No employee will do that." —PAUL COOKSON

Web appeal is just as important as curb appeal since over 90% of house buyers now start their search online. If you own a house at 2120 Washington street, then the agent should purchase the domain name www.2120washington.com and put all the information about the house on this website. There should not be any information about other listings the real estate agent has or other listings period. It should only have information about the subject property. It costs $7 - $15 to purchase a domain name so the investment is very minimal.

This website should have tabs or links to access the photos, the video, the 3D tour, the drone video, the floor plans, map, school information, etc. This website should have enough content that it keeps a potential buyer engaged with the property for an extended period of time. The goal of the website is to get a buyer to schedule a showing and to give a buyer all the information they need to make an offer after seeing the house. The website does not need to be state of the art, after all simplicity is the ultimate sophistication according to Leonardo da Vinci. Some websites can be very cutting edge but difficult to navigate if the person is not familiar with its interface. I like having a simple website with a simple visible menu that buyers can easily navigate. Here are some examples of the pages on one of my websites:

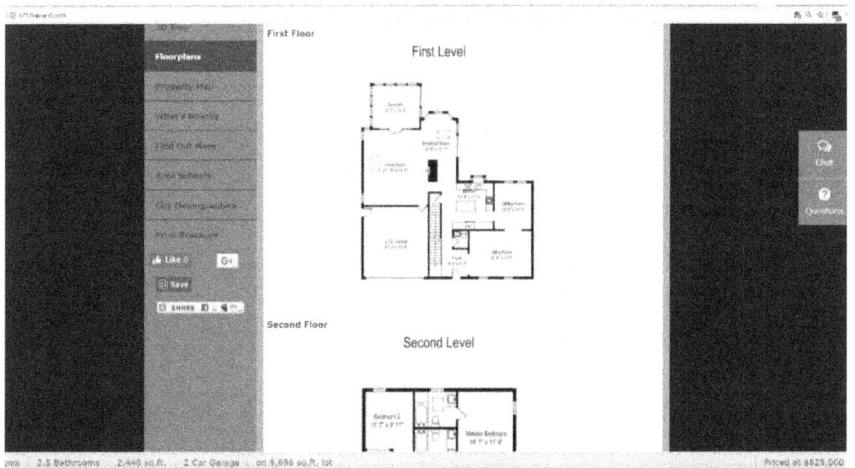

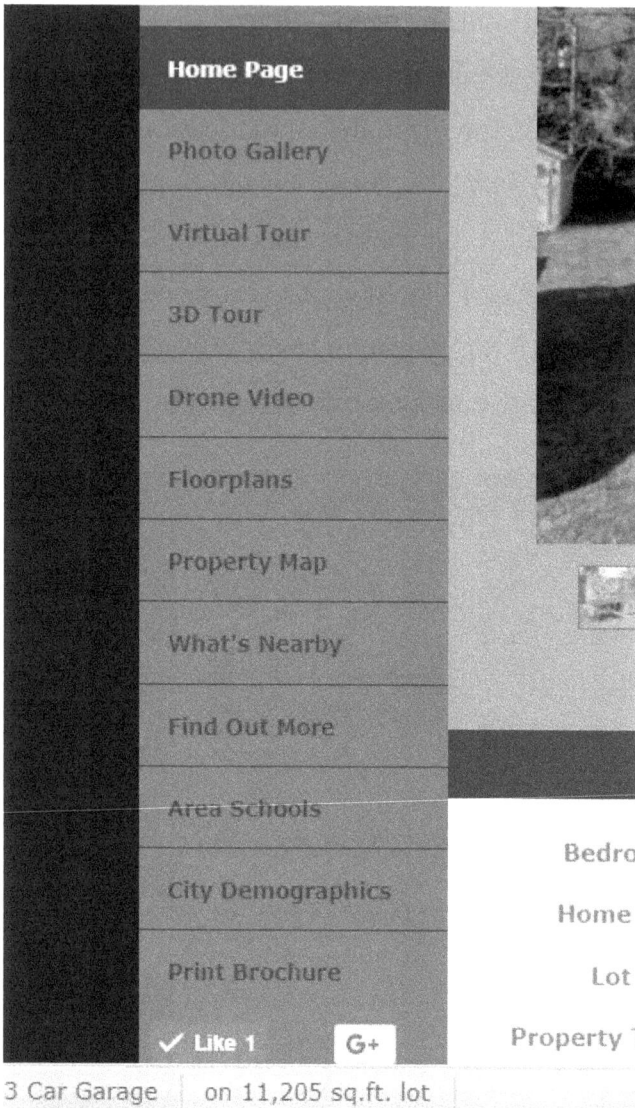

Home Page

Photo Gallery

Virtual Tour

3D Tour

Drone Video

Floorplans

Property Map

What's Nearby

Find Out More

Area Schools

City Demographics

Print Brochure

✓ Like 1   G+

Bedro

Home

Lot

Property

3 Car Garage   on 11,205 sq.ft. lot

The picture above is an example of a simple web menu for one of our listings. It is very easy for someone to navigate and click any tab to get the desired information about the property.

There is no excuse for not having a website built for a house. There are plenty of services out there that can build websites for agents. Agentmarketing.com, godaddy.com, wix.com, sitebuilder.com, web.com, webstarts.com, weebly.com, and many more.

All of the marketing that is created for the house should drive buyers to the website. The sign rider underneath the main sign panel that is placed in the yard should have the website on it so buyers that are driving by can visit the website to get more information (Read Chapter 10 for more info). Many times, a buyer does not want to talk to the listing real estate agent when they drive by, they would prefer to look at the information online. It is better to drive them to the custom website than having them look on a third-party website where other houses for sale get suggested to the buyer.

That is why the website must be mobile optimized so potential buyers that drive by can look at the website on their smart phone. A mobile optimized website is a website that displays properly on a cell phone. A report by Hitwise "examined hundreds of millions of online search queries" across PCs, smartphones and tablets between April 10 and May 7, 2016. They found that 48% of online searches for real estate/property were initiated by a mobile device! This will likely be over 50% by the time you are reading this book because mobile is trending up every year. Heck, you might even be reading this book on a tablet, kindle, or phone right now.

Still not convinced the website for your house needs to be mobile optimized? Below are two photos for the same event which show the power of cellular devices. The photo from 2005 is when Pope Benedict was elected. The photo from 2013 is when Pope Francis was elected. As you can see, mobile has trended up drastically in a short amount of time. If your real estate website is not mobile optimized, you are missing half of the market!

In Summary

Not having a custom website is a big reason why a house doesn't sell. There are thousands of third-party real estate websites like Zillow, Trulia, Realtor.com, and Redfin. These third-party websites have millions of houses listed on their platforms. When a real estate agent tells a prospective buyer to look at the listing on a third-party website, the agent is doing their clients a big disservice. When a prospective buyer goes to one of these third-party websites, a bunch of other houses listed for sale get suggested to them. They click on other listings and before you know it, they see a house that they like better than the original house they were interested in. That is why it is important to build a custom real estate website for the subject property. The custom website that is built must also be mobile optimized because more people are using their phones to browse the internet than ever before.

Now that your house has its very own website, what about your social media presence?

YOUR HOUSE IS

ANTISOCIAL

CHAPTER 7

"Social media is about people! Not about your business. Provide for the people and the people will provide for you." —MATT GOULART

Every year, people are spending more and more time on social media. The average person will spend almost two hours (approximately 116 minutes) on social media a day in 2017. That is why it is important to get your house in front of buyers while they are on these social media platforms because this is where people are spending the most time online.

YouTube

The average person spends 40 minutes a day on YouTube. If your house is not on YouTube and cannot be found on YouTube, you are missing out on the largest social media platform that people spend their time on. Not only is YouTube the largest social media platform, it is also the second largest search engine online behind Google. This means that people will most likely do a search online for something using YouTube before Yahoo or Bing. What's even more import than that is Google owns YouTube.

When you post a video to YouTube with the proper keywords, title, description, and tags, it can rank on Google in hours. Since Google owns YouTube, Google indexes videos in its search engine that are posted into YouTube very quickly.

The video(s) that should get uploaded to YouTube are the high definition videos that we talked about in Chapter 3. At least two videos should be uploaded, even if they are the same video. The agent should have a couple YouTube channels to do this.

The files and titles should be named:

Homes for Sale in City, State Zip, Unique Feature, Neighborhood, or School

X Bedroom Homes for Sale in City, State Zip, Unique Feature, Neighborhood, or School

The video should also have multiple tags below the description. Tags help people find the video on YouTube and Google when they do searches. You want to pretend like you are a buyer, what would you type into Google if you were looking to buy a house in your city? The keywords and phrases you would use to search for a house on the internet are what you want to use as tags in your YouTube video.

Also keep in mind YouTube will choose 3 parts of your video that you want to show in the thumbnail. A thumbnail is what people see before they click on a video. I recommend using a photo of the front of the house if it is the best picture but if the kitchen is spectacular, I would use that instead. You want to put your best foot forward so buyers click on your video. Below are some examples of YouTube videos we have created and the thumbnails that show for them.

Luxury Homes for Sale in Chicago | Ravenswood Manor

337 views · 1 year ago

Homes for Sale in Naperville Illinois, District 203

234 views · 1 year ago

Homes For Sale in Chicago, IL 60625 In Ravenswood

1K views · 1 year ago

Homes for sale in Chicago Illinois, Norwood Park,

58 views · 1 year ago

Homes for Sale in Chicago Illinois, 60646, Norwood

540 views · 1 year ago

Why Most Real Estate Agents Fail

133 views · 1 year ago

Pictured above: Videos on one of my YouTube channels

Facebook

The average person will spend 35 minutes a day on Facebook. If the agent you hire is not marketing on Facebook, you are missing the mark. There is a fine line that a real estate agent needs to walk on Facebook. The agent cannot always be asking for business or selling. If a real estate agent is only selling, selling, selling, people will begin to tune out that person. The formula for success on Facebook is give, give, give, give, give, ask or take. Read Jab, Jab, Jab, Right Hook by Gary Vaynerchuk to learn more about social media marketing.

The way I give each day is by posting motivational quotes on beautiful pictures. I typically get several likes and shares every single day with my quotes. Because I post every single day consistently and get likes and shares on my posts, Facebook recognizes that. Facebook then pushes my content and my posts to more and more people. Even when I am asking or taking, I still get likes and shares because people are accustomed to liking and sharing my content.

Facebook and YouTube are currently battling for video marketing. YouTube is still dominant for video content but that may change one day. The best thing about uploading videos to Facebook is that there is much less competition and less people uploading videos to Facebook. That is why the videos that I upload to Facebook usually outperform the videos I upload to YouTube 10 to 1. You do not just want to share the link from YouTube on your Facebook because Facebook is not going to share it to very many people. Facebook wants to promote its own platform so you must upload the videos you create to Facebook as well. I typically get several hundred views on every single video I upload to Facebook and thousands of views is not unusual either.

What is very powerful about Facebook is that I can run advertisements that target buyers that are likely to move in certain zip codes around the house. I can also target buyers that make a certain income level so I am hitting buyers that can afford the house as well. How does Facebook know how much money a person makes? It is kind of scary but Facebook data-mines the information from all the websites a person visits and builds a profile on you and tracks your spending habits.

La Grange Homes For Sale Luxury - 1032 S Spring
February 24 · ⊘

Watch a high def video of this dream home which features 4 levels of living space measuring at 5,729 sqft not including the finished basement! Visit www.1032spring.com to learn more

La Grange Homes For Sale

Send Message

15,932 people reached

↻ View Results

8.6K Views

Pictured above: With a $100 advertisement, this video reached 15,932 people and had over 8,000 views!

Even better, a Facebook fan page can be created for the subject house! Just like a website, this Facebook page will have photos, video, a link to the 3D virtual tour and more. The house can be shared easily on social media by the real estate agent, the seller, friends, and family. The best part of it is that the marketing that is created for the house is in one place and your house can have a unique URL on Facebook once you get a certain amount of likes for the page.

How powerful is Facebook? Very powerful! Many businesses do not advertise their websites anymore on commercials and will promote their Facebook pages over websites for people to interact with them and stay engaged. This is especially staggering when many of these companies spent thousands of dollars to create state of the art websites. That is why your house should also have a URL on Facebook.

For a couple of examples of Facebook pages that I have created visit:

https://www.facebook.com/norwoodparkhomes/

https://www.facebook.com/lagrangehomesforsale/

LinkedIn

People do not spend as much time on LinkedIn as they do for YouTube or Facebook but according to the Content Marketing Institute 66% of marketers ranked LinkedIn as their most effective content marketing platform! It is the biggest B2B (business to business) platform and advertising your business and properties for sale is very welcome here. That is why I have spent every single day the last 7 years building up my LinkedIn profile to an All Star level (according to LinkedIn).

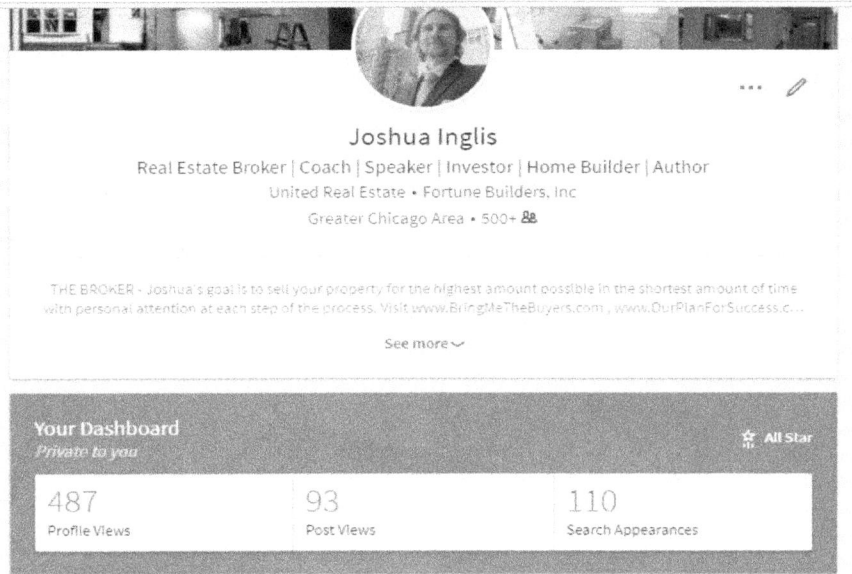

Pictured above: My LinkedIn profile

LinkedIn is great because you can write a blog article about the house with photos, video, floor plans, and a link to the 3D tour. The article can be as long or as short as you want but you do not want it to be boring or people will stop opening the blog articles.

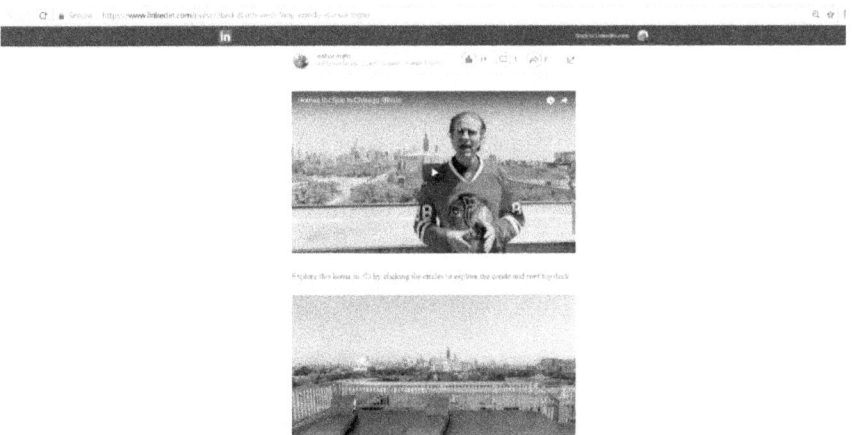

Pictured above: Article I created on LinkedIn for one of my listings

You can also just do a posting on LinkedIn which is much quicker than an article and people that are connected to you will see the post without having to click the article to see what it's about. If I do a posting, I usually do the video or 3D tour with a short description of the house and a link to the website so buyers can get more information. Below is an example of how to get a lot of eyeballs on your house for free using a LinkedIn post.

Pictured above: One of my posts on LinkedIn for one of my listings

In Summary

You want to make sure your house is on the big 3 social media platforms: YouTube, Facebook, and LinkedIn. All 3 of the platforms are free to use and will help give your house maximum exposure where people are spending the most time online. For YouTube, you want to make sure the video is titled correctly with the right description and has the right tags so it gets found organically by potential buyers. Your house can have its very own Facebook fan page which is easily shareable with all the photos, 3d tour, videos, etc. Your house should have its own Facebook.com domain like www.facebook.com/shortdescriptionofhouse . For a small budget of $100, your house can be shown to thousands of buyers likely to move that make a certain income level. LinkedIn is great for posting videos of your house and for writing articles with all the photos, 3d tour, videos, etc.

Twitter, Instagram, Pinterest, and Google+ are also used by my team to advertise houses but they are not as powerful as the big 3 for now. Until other social media platforms take more market share, they should be used but not focused on like YouTube, Facebook, and LinkedIn to market a house.

Now that your house has a great web and social media presence, what about print marketing?

YOUR HOUSE DOESN'T HAVE
PRINT MARKETING
CHAPTER 8

"Make it simple. Make it memorable. Make it inviting to look at. Make it fun to read." —LEO BURNETT

Print marketing for your house is a wonderful form of promotion that should be created in all shapes and sizes so potential buyers can take it in a size that is convenient for them.

Studies have shown that people view high quality print advertising longer than digital advertising. People on the internet click through sites and ads at a very fast rate vs. when someone is holding a tangible piece of print marketing. People also remember physical advertising for a longer period of time and can recall details better than digital marketing. Print marketing creates a stronger emotional response to the house which triggers a greater intent to purchase in the brain.

That is why you will want to create the following types of print marketing for your house

Door Hangers

Door hangers are a convenient way to inform the neighborhood that your house is for sale. Someone from the neighborhood probably knows a buyer that may want to move into the area whether that is a friend, a family member, or a co-worker. Sometimes it may be a neighbor that is looking for a house for themselves whether it's bigger, smaller, or a rental property since it is convenient to manage close by. The door hanger is a great way to get the word out that the house is for sale. I was out putting door hangers on neighborhood houses on a new listing I just acquired and a nice lady that lived directly behind the house I was selling didn't know that the family I was representing were selling. This was especially astounding to me because this was a listing that another agent failed to sell for 10 months! No wonder the house didn't sell, no one knew it was for sale! The previous agent failed to give the house the proper exposure to the area that the house deserved and nothing is more effective of getting the word out then grass roots marketing!

Leave Behind Flyers

These are large full-size flyers in high quality print that are created about the house. If buyers have interest in a property they will take one or a couple of these flyers. These are great to have for open houses and should always be available for buyers to take from private showings with their real estate agent. The flyers should be placed in an easily visible location. If the subject house is vacant, I will put the flyers throughout the house in the master bedroom, master bathroom, kitchen counter, and living room. If the house is lived in and you have a small decorative table in your foyer, it is a great place to put the flyers. It's something you want buyers to see right when they walk in if possible so they grab it right away and keep it with them the entire time.

Marketing Flyers

These are smaller flyers about a third of the size of a leave behind flyer. These are great for putting up on bulletin boards at grocery stores or coffee shops. I also leave them at open houses for buyers to take because sometimes buyers don't want to take a full size flyer and a smaller flyer is easier to put in a purse or in a pocket.

Business Cards

You should have business cards created for your house as well. These are the most convenient size so you can hand them out to literally anyone. These are great to hand out to people that know someone looking to move into the area. Instead of giving them a huge flyer, a business card can be easily put into a wallet.

MLS Data Sheet

The MLS data sheet has all types of information about the house like bedroom and bathroom count, room sizes, flooring type, tax information, etc. The more information that is filled out for the data sheet the better. This should be printed out and put with your high-quality print flyers so buyers can take it with them and gives specifics regarding the house. The analytical types will always take the data sheets and so will interested buyers.

Pictured above: Typical professional print marketing my team creates for one of our listings which include door hangers, leave behind flyers, marketing flyers, business cards, and more.

In Summary

Every house that is for sale should have professional print marketing that is created in all shapes and sizes from small to large. It creates a stronger emotional response for buyers and keeps your house in front of potential buyers long after a showing or open house.

Now that your house has great print advertising, how do you get the word out to the community that your house is for sale with print?

YOUR HOUSE DOESN'T HAVE
A GROUND GAME
CHAPTER 9

"Stopping advertising to save money is like stopping your watch to save time." —HENRY FORD

You must have information about your house hit the mailboxes in the community to give your house maximum exposure. You want as many buyers as possible to know your house is for sale and direct mail is one of the best forms of grass roots marketing to do that. Direct mail gets a much higher response rate than other forms of marketing and people look at print advertising longer than digital advertising as we discussed in the last chapter.

Don't just take my word for it, according to the United States Direct Marketing Association 42 percent of recipients read or scanned the mail pieces that they received. They also found that the response rate of direct mail pieces is 3.7% compared to 2% mobile, 1% social media, and 0.2% internet display.

A study done by the Canada Post "The neuroscience behind the response-driving power of direct mail. July 31, 2015" found that:

- Direct mail is easier to understand and more memorable than digital media. It requires 21% less cognitive effort to process and elicits a much higher brand recall.
- Direct mail is more persuasive than digital media. Its motivation response is 20% higher and even higher if it appeals to additional senses beyond touch.
- Direct mail is visually processed quicker in the brain and the message comes across faster than digital media.
- Most importantly, direct mail is more likely to drive some sort of response than digital media. This means it gets buyers to take action!
  o The motivation-to-cognitive load ratio for direct mail is 1.1
  o The motivation-to-cognitive load ratio for digital media is 0.87

See the entire study by visiting https://www.canadapost.ca/assets/pdf/blogs/CPC_Neuroscience_EN_150717.pdf

But my neighbor is not going to buy my house...

This can't be further from the truth because 17 out of 20 times, the buyer for your house or buyer's friends/family live within a five mile radius of your house. Grass roots marketing is powerful because it gets your house in front of people in the community who know a buyer who wants to move into the neighborhood. Sometimes one of the neighbors is looking to buy another house in the neighborhood for themselves (bigger or smaller), their kids, or is looking for an investment property. That is why it is extremely important to market your house locally to buyers in the community within a five mile radius.

How to send a lot of mail for not a lot of money...

The problem most agents have with sending direct mail is there is a cost associated with it. A first-class stamp costs 49 cents and a postcard stamp costs 34 cents at the time I wrote this book. Don't forget there is a cost to print the marketing as well, especially if you use a professional printer like I do. This means that direct mail can become very expensive very quickly if done the traditional way. That is why I use Every Door Direct Mail (EDDM). It allows me to send a large quantity of direct mail to a geographic region for 16 cents per piece (not including printing costs). This is how I am able to send 1,000 – 2,000 mailers on all of my listings.

Saturate the Market

Is direct mail marketing better than internet marketing? The answer is yes and no. I believe both are equally important to sell a house. I never put all of my eggs in one basket and neither should you. You want potential buyers to see your house on the internet, on social media, and through direct mail. You want to completely saturate a market with information about your house both digitally and physically.

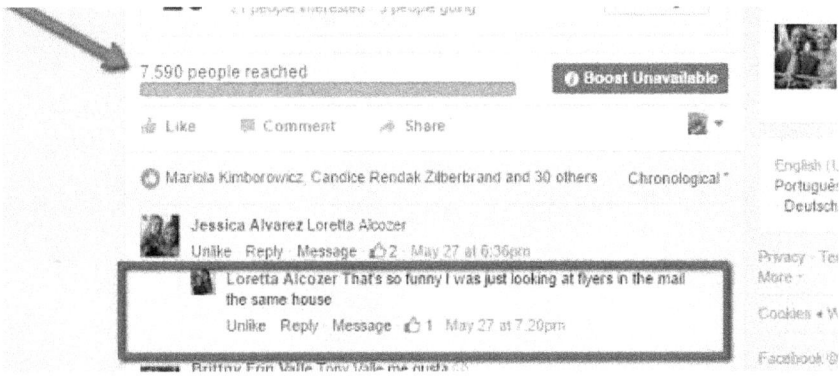

Pictured above: Screenshot from Facebook showing how social media and mailers worked together to completely saturate a market with my client's house.

In Summary

Direct mail is an integral part of selling your house for the most amount of money in the shortest amount of time and gives the house maximum exposure to the area. Many agents will say that print advertisement is dead for the simple reason the agent does not want to spend the money but it cannot be farther from the truth. Not having a ground game is a sure way to not sell your house. That is why direct mail should always be a part of a real estate agents marketing plan to sell your house.

Now that you have great print advertising and mailings, what about the signage?

YOUR HOUSE DOESN'T HAVE A
GOOD BILLBOARD
CHAPTER 10

"Business has only two functions – marketing and innovation." —MILAN KUNDERA

You want as many buyers as possible to know your house is for sale and the most fundamental way to do that is with a for sale sign. You should have clear signage outside the house letting everyone know the house is for sale so buyers can easily contact you or the agent. You want to have your sign on a freshly painted post that is at least 5 to 6 feet in the air. This makes it very easy for buyers that are driving by to see that your house is for sale. The higher the better so the sign has more visibility. Think of the real estate sign in your front yard as a billboard advertisement for your house so visibility is key.

You will want to put the sign up in the yard even before it is listed in the MLS if possible. I have sold houses before we even took photos because someone from the area saw the sign in the yard and either called or told someone else about it. That is why it is a good idea to get the sign in the yard with a "Coming Soon" rider above the sign as soon as possible. This gets people in the neighborhood excited and talking about the house to create a buzz before it is even listed.

The real estate sign itself should be very simple with the words FOR SALE at the top in all capital letters. The sign an agent uses should have their company logo and team logo on the sign, the agents name, the agents phone number, and the agents photo. The sign should be professionally made because if the sign looks cheap, buyers will subconsciously associate a cheap sign with a cheap property. That is why the sign and the post must both be in good condition. I have a black sign with white font because it really stands out compared to other signs and many times buyers associate black signs with luxury.

Sign Rider

Underneath the sign there should be a rider so buyers can get more information about your house without having to call the real estate agent. Many people would rather eat a box of nails then speak to a real estate agent so having multiple ways of getting information is important.

The sign rider should have the URL to the website that was built for your house that is mobile optimized (www.youraddress.com). In Chapter 6 we discussed the importance of having a website so buyers do not go to Zillow, Trulia, Realtor.com, etc. where after they look up your house, other houses get suggested to them. Rather, we want buyers to go to a website with your house and your house exclusively. We have lots of content built on these sites so we keep potential buyers engaged with the photos, videos, 3D tour, floor plans, what's nearby, etc.

The sign rider should also have a 24-hour text line that buyers can text to get more information. If a buyer texts the number, all the information, the price, and website get sent to their phones. The best part about the 24-hour text line is that the real estate agent is able to capture the potential buyer's information and follow up with a phone call to see if they have any further questions. I also have a preferred lender follow up with them to see if they are pre-qualified to purchase the house and get the process started if they are not.

Lastly, the sign rider should have a QR code that potential buyers can scan with a QR scanner. This is especially important for millennials who are tech savvy and have a QR scanner application on their phone. Once a person scans the QR code, all the information for the house gets instantly sent to their phone and they can view the website.

ON THE WEB AND ON YOUR PHONE
www.1032spring.com
TEXT: "SpringAve" TO: 79564

Pictured above: A sample sign rider from one of my listings.

Construction Signage

My team works with real estate developers and one of the most important things to a developer is how quickly a property or development will sell. One of the most important things to have while construction is going on is to have very good signage to promote the property specific to the development. The sign should be installed as early as possible in the construction process, even if it is just land. This is a way to pre-market the property before completion. Many times, a buyer will be found from the sign before the house or development is even finished. Each city has rules and regulations regarding how big the sign can be but we always try to install the biggest sign that is allowed. This sign should have information about the developer, a website for more information, a 24-hour text line, a QR code, and a way to contact to the agent. We have these signs custom made for each development project.

Pictured above: Custom 4ft by 8ft sign for this house during construction

In Summary

In order to give your house maximum exposure to the marketplace, you want to have a real estate sign that is easily visible to buyers driving by. The sign should be put in the yard as early as possible with a coming soon rider above the sign to create buzz. An additional rider should be installed below the sign with the website, 24-hour text line, and QR code. This gives potential buyers 4 ways to get information about the house (phone, web, text, and mobile application) so that the house is engaged in a way that the potential buyer wants to get the information. If you are a developer, the real estate agent should get a custom sign designed and installed at the construction site so that the subject property/development can be presold before completion.

Now that you have a good billboard outside the house, how does the house look inside?

YOUR HOUSE IS
A MESS

CHAPTER 11

"One of the most glorious messes in the world is the mess created in the living room on Christmas day. Don't clean it up too quickly."—ANDY ROONEY

You want to make sure you house is as clean and clutter free as possible. You want to make all the rooms look spacious. If rooms are full of clutter, they will look smaller than they really are. That is why it is important to meet with a professional stager in cases where you are not clear of what should be removed from the house. As a general rule of thumb, about 50% of your personal belongings should be removed from the house.

Read chapter 5 for staging tips but you will want to remove items and furniture from the house that break up the flow. If something is intruding in the walking path from the dining room into the family room for example, remove it. I have my professional stager meet with my clients to go over what should stay and what should be removed because sometimes it is a difficult decision for a homeowner to make. It is always good to have a professional third-party objective opinion on matters like these. The presentation of your house needs to be as appealing as possible to potential buyers. It is a very good idea to rent a storage unit to move some of the "clutter" from the house. If you do not plan on keeping some of the items/furniture for the future, Goodwill or Salvation Army are great places to donate these items. You will be amazed at how roomy and nice the house feels after all the clutter has been removed

The house should also be as neutral as possible. Personal photos should be put out of sight. You do not want potential buyers to see photos of your family in the house, you want potential buyers to envision themselves and their family living in the house which is hard to do if you have photos of your family throughout.

After the house has been decluttered and the personal photos have been removed it is time to clean! You want your house to be as clean as possible and shine for showings so buyers associate your house with the words "well maintained" or "pride of ownership" vs "deferred maintenance".

As an example, your car has probably never been as clean inside as it was when you purchased it from the car dealership. Very few people would pay $20,000 or more for a car from a dealership if there was trash, dirt, and grime inside of it. Car dealerships understand that clean sells and if they clean a used car to a point where it looks new again, they can get top dollar for that car. That is why car dealerships do an impeccable job at detailing and cleaning a car before they sell it. The same principles apply to selling a house, clean means green dollar signs.

You should clean your house from top to bottom, literally. Start from the top cleaning cobwebs because they will fall to the ground and onto your furniture and flooring. You will want to dust the ceiling fans, and clean all of the light fixtures. If you have any flush mount lights, remove the cover and clean because flies can sometimes get in them and are visible to buyers. Dust the blinds or replace them if they cannot be cleaned (paper ones will turn yellow over time). If the curtains are dirty, clean them as well or replace them.

Wash the walls, remove all grease and splatters. Mr Clean makes a product called the Magic Eraser which is the best investment you can make to remove stains, scuff marks, and dirt on the walls. It is the next best thing you can do next to repainting a room. Even if you plan to paint a room, it is a good idea to clean the walls first. Prepping the walls is the single most important step when painting. "Give me six hours to chop down a tree and I will spend the first four sharpening the axe." - Abraham Lincoln

You will want to clean all the glass in your house which includes the windows, the glass in the doors, the tv's, mirrors, glass tables, etc. If you have wooden surfaces and furniture, you will want to polish them.

You will want to vacuum the furniture and wipe down the leather couches with a leather cleaning and conditioning product.

You want to clean out and reorganize the closets and cabinets. If you haven't worn something in the last 6 months, get rid of it or put it into storage. It is ideal to put all of your clothes on wooden hangers in the master bedroom closet, it makes the closet feel more luxurious.

You want to make the appliances shine like they did when they were brand new at the store if you are not planning on replacing them. This includes cleaning the inside of the appliances as well, nobody wants to buy a house with a smelly fridge, stove, or microwave. The best trick we have found for cleaning stove burners and grates effortlessly is with ammonia. You can put the grates and burners in a large black trash bag with ammonia and leave it in the sunlight outside for a few hours. You can then rub off the grease right back into the bag with a sponge. It removes the grease effortlessly and keeps the mess contained within the trash bag. If you have stainless steel appliances, you will want to purchase Weiman Stainless Steel Cleaner and Polish, it will make the appliances look amazing.

The kitchen and bathrooms need to be impeccably clean, eat off the floor clean to be exact. Someone may forgive a less than stellar cleaned kids room but the kitchen and bathroom must be perfect because no one is going to pay top dollar for a house with a grungy kitchen or bathroom. This means cleaning counters, faucets, sinks, toilets, showers, and tiles. You will want to replace any caulking or grout with mildew or discoloration. Replacing a toilet seat can go a long way and is an inexpensive solution.

If you have hardwood floors that no longer shine, you do not necessarily need to spend the money to refinish them unless they are in really bad shape with gouges. There is an amazing product I have found to make hardwood look amazing again and it is Scott's Liquid Gold which can be purchased at Home Depot and other hardware stores. The hardwood floors will look almost as good as if they were refinished.

You will want to vacuum and shampoo the carpets as well. You may need to professionally steam clean the carpets with a company like Stanley Steemer if there are stains that you cannot get out yourself. If the carpets still have really bad stains or an odor even after steam cleaning, you will probably want to replace the carpet and pad. Read the next chapter to learn more about odors.

The mechanical room is often overlooked with the furnace, water heater, and sump pump. Many times people have rust on the water heater pipe connections and don't even realize it. Purchase a wire brush and make the metal connections shine like new and vacuum up the rust. Sometimes rust can be found on furnaces as well so make sure to clean that up as well. Something that most people overlook commonly is the furnace filter, replace it even it doesn't need to be replaced in your opinion. I have been on showings where a buyer looks at the furnace and pulls the filter out partially to see if its dirty. If a buyer sees a dirty filter, they think the owner of the house did not care for the furnace and the house has other deferred maintenance issues. Replace the furnace filter every single month during the showing process. Make sure there is no standing water in the mechanical room whatsoever from the sump pump, loose connection on the washer, etc.

In Summary

If you want to sell your house about 50% of your belongings should be given to charity, sold, or put into storage. The less clutter you have in the house the better. You will also want to keep the house clean, tidy, and sparkling. You want buyers to associate your house with the words "well maintained".

Now that the house is spick and span, what about that smell?

YOUR HOUSE
STINKS
CHAPTER 12

"Guests, like fish, begin to smell after three days."
—BENJAMIN FRANKLIN

You want your house to smell like **HOME** when someone walks into the front door. That is why I recommend baking cookies or an apple pie before a showing when possible (be careful not to burn them or this will back fire). I will sometimes bake an apple pie at my open houses because I want to appeal to all of the senses for a potential buyer. One of the first things that buyers mention when they walk in the door of a house where we are baking a pie is how wonderful the house smells. It gives buyers a great first impression and follows them throughout the entire house and showing process.

Houses with bad odors on the other hand are extremely difficult to sell and no one wants to think that they have a smelly house. Smoke odors, strong cooking smells, pet odors, and stale mildew odors are all deal breakers for the majority of buyers out there. If you tried listing your house in the past and received feedback that your house had a bad odor or smell more than twice, I would take that under very serious consideration. Most buyers do not want to offend anyone by leaving feedback that a house smells so if you received it twice, you probably had several other buyers think that but they did not say it or give feedback. I have seen sellers become very offended when the subject is brought up so potential buyers will not always give that kind of feedback to avoid confrontation or do not want to seem harsh. That is why your house must not only be clean but also smell clean.

Smoke Odors

Fewer people are smoking these days and smoking is banned from all commercial flights, most restaurants, hotels, bowling alleys, and bars. This means that buyers are exposed to smoke odors less than ever before. Non-smokers are more sensitive to the smell because they are not exposed to it as often as they were in the past. Smoke odors are very hard to get rid of because smoke will seep into clothes, coats, drapes, curtains, walls, and carpeting. If you are smoking anywhere in the house right now and you are trying to sell your house, you need to stop! I don't mean stop smoking completely, I mean stop smoking in the house. Even the garage is not a good place to smoke because it will come into the house, you should smoke outside or in your car.

Now that I have stated the obvious about smoking in the house, you need to remove the smoking smells. You need to remove all sources of smoke which include cigarette butts, ashtrays, cigars, etc. Tie them up in a grocery bag and place them outside in an outdoor trash bin. You will want to air out the house by opening as many windows as possible and point fans towards the windows to increase airflow. You will want to purchase deodorizing products that do not just mask the smoke smell but get rid of it. The products that will eliminate the smell will contain baking soda, activated charcoal, or hydrogen peroxide.

You will next want to gather all of cloths and linens (clothing, pillows, curtains, etc.) Wash all of them, yes all of them! If certain items need to be dry cleaned vs washed then you will have to dry clean them. If you do not want to rack up an enormous dry cleaning bill, you should store these clothing items outside of the house until the house is sold. Take down the curtains and shades and wash them because they are ideal spots for tar and resin to settle and permeate into.

You will definitely need to shampoo or steam clean your carpet. You can also sprinkle liberal amounts of baking soda on your carpet and let it soak for a day. You can then vacuum the following day and this may take several applications. If it does not work to remove the odor from the carpet, you want to consider replacing the carpet. You can also use baking soda on fabric covered furniture or use a chemical cleaner like OdoBan.

To clean non-fabric surfaces like floors, ceilings, window screens, walls, cabinets, furniture, etc. you will want to use diluted bleach or distilled white vinegar. If there is a strong smell from the closet, you will want to remove all the clothes in order to clean the closet walls and ceiling.

If the walls still have an odor after a couple cleanings, you may need to repaint the house with a deodorizing primer product like Zinsser Bullseye and Kilz which can be purchased at any hardware store. You may even need to do a couple coats of paint with Bullseye and Kilz if the smell is still lingering.

One thing you may want to try before repainting the house is renting an ozone generator machine. This is what hotels use to remove odors. You will want to run the machine for several hours which creates a fog or mist to kill odors and you cannot be present while it runs. You will want to run it on each level of the house.

Strong Cooking Odors

If you are a master chef and cook/fry fish frequently or use strong spices like curry or cumin you might have a problem selling your house. I have been in houses where the cooking smell is so strong, it can be smelled in the basement and second level. This can be a problem for buyers and I have been with several clients where they mention they love the house but are not interested due to the strong cooking smell. I tell the clients that the smell can be removed but the clients do not want the hassle or take the risk they cannot remove the odor. I have even had clients walk into houses and walk immediately back out just because of a strong cooking odor. You do not want this to happen to your house.

To remove cooking odors you will want to wash all the surfaces in the house where cooking smells are present with a Vinegar/water solution (One cup of water, Two Tablespoons of white vinegar). Spray the walls and give extra attention to the kitchen area. Make sure to thoroughly spray/clean the microwave, stove and around the stove (backsplash, under stove, behind stove, range hood) and any area where oil vapors could hide. Keep the windows open to let the house air-dry. After you have cleared out the cooking odors, you will want to cook as little as possible. If cooking is a must while you are trying to sell the house, cook conservatively with no strong spices or fish, absolutely no frying!

Pet Odors

Before I go any further in this section I want you to know that I love animals. I love animals so much that I currently have 3 rescue pets. With that being said, dogs and cats have accidents and leave odors. I am not saying this to offend you in any way but it is true no matter how diligent you are with your pets. Every pet will have an accident at some point but you do not want your house to smell like your pets. Why? Because I have been in houses with dog and cat odors which are deal breakers for the new buyers.

You want to vacuum daily or every other day if you have pets. I recommend you purchasing a Dyson Animal vacuum, it is the best investment I have ever made to keep my house clean. It is amazing how much hair and dust it pulls up. You want to vacuum floors, baseboards, carpets, rugs, furniture, under furniture, cushions, and areas where the pets spend a lot of time.

You will want to purchase an enzyme cleaner. Usually hidden or improperly cleaned messes are usually the culprit for pet odors in your house. You will want to revisit some of these areas and let the cleaner soak for 30 minutes and then blot it dry with a clean cloth. To find some of these hidden messes, you should purchase a black light and go throughout the entire house when it is dark. Night time is best with the lights off to find hidden messes (please be careful). If there are pet messes on the trim or wood work, you may have to replace it in order to fully eliminate the odors.

Make sure to clean the furniture regularly especially if your pet has a favorite couch or chair they like to sleep in. Clean your pet's bed regularly. Most pet beds can be machine washed and larger ones typically have a removeable cover. Next clean your bed. While linens are being washed, sprinkle baking soda on your mattress. Wait for 30 minutes to an hour and then vacuum it up.

Give your pet regular baths which is very important for dogs and less regular bathing is ok for cats. Some pets hate being bathed but is necessary in the odor elimination process.

If you have cats, you will want to clean the litterbox with a scooper at least twice a day during the showing process and preferably before showings. You also must be diligent about cleaning the actual litterbox because many times odors can get trapped on the sides of the box. You will want to remove the cat litter once a week or every couple weeks at a minimum and use vinegar and let it soak for about 30 minutes. Then scrub the box clean and rinse it out. Let the box completely dry and then use fresh cat litter.

Clean your pets cage regularly as well if it is used. If you have mice, ferrets, gerbils, rabbits, turtles, fish, etc. you will want to clean the cage or tank before showings begin. It is a tedious process but necessary because you don't want buyers to refer to your house as the "smelly house".

Before each showing if possible, you will want to open the windows an hour before to give your house fresh air. Don't leave all the windows open during the showing process either because that may raise red flags. You may also want to invest in an air purifier which will help with odors. Lastly, do not overuse air fresheners because that can turn buyers off as well. I've had potential buyers not purchase a house simply because the homeowner overdid it with the air freshener and the buyer thought they were trying to hide something.

Musty, Mildew, or Stale Odors

If a house is vacant and does not get regular air circulation, it may begin to get a musty, mildew, or stale smell. For this reason, it is always a good idea to leave a window somewhere in the house open a crack if the house is vacant. I usually recommend people to do this in an upstairs bathroom that is not accessible from the ground or a very small window that no one can climb into. You want to make sure the window is in a place where rain is not going to come into the house. Baking soda is your best friend if your house is musty and you can strategically place it throughout the house but so it is not visible. You can also leave an open box of baking soda in an area for a few days and then remove it.

Appliances like fridges can smell really terrible if left empty. You will want to clean them with a white vinegar solution or use baking soda. It is always a good idea to leave a box of baking soda in the fridge whether it has an odor or not.

When cleaning hard furniture like tables you will want to use chlorine dioxide to get rid of musty smells. Soft furniture and carpet you will want to use hydrogen peroxide or baking soda to eliminate stale odors

Many times, the smell comes from the basement or other damp areas like a crawl space. You will want to air it out as frequently as possible and use potpourri to absorb odors. Make sure to use a dehumidifier as well to eliminate any dampness from the basement. You will want to remove the dehumidifier from the basement for showings though so it does not raise red flags. Sometimes buyers think that a basement has flooding issues if a dehumidifier is present during showings. You will also want to seal the sump pump with a cover, sometimes odors can originate from the sump pump pit.

In Summary

You want your house to smell like a HOME and not like a cigar shop, animal shelter, fish market, or damp basement. No one wants to buy the "smelly house" that they visited when they looked at several other houses that did not smell. The odor doesn't even need to be drastic like I described in the first sentence of this paragraph and it will still deter buyers with an acute sense of smell or a buyer with allergies.

If you tried selling your house in the past and received feedback that your house had an odor you will want to take it under very serious consideration. Many people are hesitant to give such feedback so it can be a deal breaker for a lot of buyers. Keeping the house as odor free as possible will be key to sell your house for the most amount of money in the shortest amount of time.

Now that your house is clean and smells wonderful, how easy is it for buyers to visit the house in person?

YOU HAVE A
CLOSED HOUSE
CHAPTER 13

"80% of success is just showing up." —WOODY ALLEN

You want to make sure that your house is available to show to all qualified potential buyers within relatively short notice. Many times a buyer will only go out with their agent two or three times before making a decision to buy. I have been out with different buyer clients where we go out to look at houses only once and a decision is made the first time out. We may only look at 2-4 houses on that day and if the buyer really likes a house, they will make an offer on one of them. If you are unable to accommodate a showing request remember that it could have been the person that was going to buy your house. A potential buyer will not reschedule if they find something else they like that day or if they are not coming back to that area on the next trip out. Buyers might look at houses in one town or area on one day and look at houses in another town or area on the next time out so they won't come back to see your house on the next time out.

If your house has very limited viewing hours, it will be extremely difficult to sell. One example that comes to mind was a listing I saw in my market that stated the only showing times were: Tuesday and Thursday from 1pm to 3pm. Houses with limited showing times are extremely difficult houses to sell because many buyers also have limited times to view houses themselves. It is already difficult enough to arrange a time that works for the husband, the wife, the kids, the babysitter, the mother-in-law, and/or the agent. If a listing does not allow showings when the buyers are available to look at houses, that listing will never be seen in person or considered by the potential buyers. Houses with very limited viewing hours are also candidates for low ball offers because investor buyers know that a house that is very difficult to show is not going to get a lot of traffic.

You will also want to make as many rooms in the house accessible for buyers to view. I have been in houses where a basement or 2 or 3 rooms are locked and we are unable to view them. My buyers have made comments like "I wonder what they are hiding". It does not give a buyer the warm-and-fuzzy feeling when they cannot get into rooms because a buyer's imagination can go wild thinking maybe there is water damage in a room or something perhaps even worse.

Open Houses

There is research from the National Association of Realtors®
that indicates open houses are underrated when it comes to
their potential selling value. While most buyers search online
for houses, they will want to see the house in person before
making the decision to buy. That is why making the house
available for the public to view is very important. At a
minimum, you want to have an open house on the weekend
that the property is first listed.

Here are some different scenarios that I have personally
encountered and why open houses are important:

Example 1: The potential buyer may not be working with a
buyer's real estate agent and they may not want to reach out
to the listing agent. This means that an open house may be
the only opportunity for that potential buyer to see the house.
If the listing agent does not host an open house, the potential
buyer will never see the house which means they will never
have an opportunity to make an offer.

Example 2: The potential buyer might be working with a
buyer's real estate agent but that agent is extremely busy or
on vacation and might not be available to show the house
right away. If the agent cannot show the house to the very
interested buyer for a couple weeks, this means the house
might sit on the market for another couple weeks. The house

becomes less desirable the longer it is on the market and increases the negotiation power for the buyer.

Example 3: The potential buyer does not go to the open house themselves but a family member or friend from the area does. The friend/family member communicates information to the potential buyer about this great house that they saw at an open house. The potential buyer then reaches out to the agent they are working with or the listing agent to schedule a showing to see the house. If they love the house as much as the friend/family member did, they make an offer.

Example 4: The potential buyer might be driving through the area on their way home and are in the market to buy a house but might not be set up on a search to look in this neighborhood or area that this house is located in. While driving, the potential buyer sees the open house sign and decides to check it out. They come to the open house and fall in love with it.

Example 5: A real estate agent lives in the neighborhood where the open house is happening and decides to pop in to say hi to the listing agent or is curious about the latest house on the market in their neighborhood. After the real estate agent sees the house, they know a client who the house would be perfect for.

This makes open houses far more valuable than most people give them credit for.

WAYS TO OPTIMIZE YOUR OPEN HOUSE

All Signs Lead to Home

Put up lots of directional signs that point buyers in the right direction to get to the open house. You will want to place the directional signs starting with busy streets and intersections. This gets buyers from outside the neighborhood to attend the open house. You can even put balloons on the directional signs so it stands out for people that are driving by.

It should also be clear when buyers pull up to the house that an open house is happening. We use a six-foot flag that says open house and a directional sign pointing to the front door. This makes it very clear for potential buyers that an open house is happening. If it is not very clear to someone that an open house is happening, most buyers will not come up to the house in fear of disrupting someone at home.

Clean it Up

Read chapter 11 for house cleaning tips but you want the house to appear neat and tidy. Cleaning and decluttering the house is something that the real estate agent cannot do for you unless the house is vacant. Anything that is unsightly should be removed from the property so that you can properly present your house. In creating the best first impression, you should start with presenting a very neat and clean house that will impress visitors.

Neutralize the Personality

Another step is to remove anything that personalizes the house starting with pictures, photos and any knick-knacks or items that create the impression that the house still reflects your unique personal tastes. Instead, you'll want to present a house that is a blank slate so that potential buyers can see their own belongings inside.

Bake Cookies or a Pie

This is the oldest trick in the book but it's effective, bake cookies or a pie before your guests arrive so that the house smells like home. You can even serve the cookies as treats while potential buyers are exploring it. In addition, you'll want to get rid of any odors with neutral cleaners. Read chapter 12 about de-odorizing a house.

Sellers Should Be Away from the House

The real estate agent should host the open house and the seller should not be present. This is because a seller can be intimidating to a potential buyer and may make a buyer uncomfortable. Always schedule the open house during a time in which all the occupants are away.

Get Feedback

To really optimize your open house, every person that comes in the house should fill out a survey (Bribe people to fill it out by giving them a $5 Starbucks gift card, it works!) The survey should have questions about what buyers liked and what buyers didn't like about the house. The survey should also ask if the house is priced correctly so that you can get honest feedback from potential buyers. Several surveys that say a house is overpriced is extremely valuable to help determine if you are positioned correctly in the marketplace.

Have Fun

If you want to attract millennials or the neighbors to your open house, turn it into a party! A party can draw a large audience and create competition among buyers. You can do fun things like:

- Hire a DJ
- Serve ice cream or gelato and rent an ice cream truck for an even bigger effect

Pictured above: Renting an ice cream truck for one of our open houses

- Barbeque or hold a pool party in the summer
- Rent an inflatable bouncy house
- Host a poetry night
- Do an art auction
- Do a murder mystery at the house
- Host a chamber of commerce meeting or ribbon cutting at the house (lots of people from the town will be in attendance and will let friends, family, coworkers know about the house)

Pictured above: Chamber of Commerce ribbon cutting at one of our houses.

Your number one goal is to create an inviting atmosphere in the house. The agent should capture all the contact information from the visitors so that they can follow up with them. This is key, as a follow up call just might be what sways them to make the purchase.

In Summary

You need to make your house as accessible to qualified buyers as possible. If it is difficult to show your house, it is going to be extremely difficult to sell. Buyers may decide to purchase a house on the first, second, or third time out with their agent. If they are unable to view your house on the day it is requested, they may buy something else when they would have purchased your house if they had been able to see it. You also want to have open houses to make your house available to buyers that may not be able to view it with their agent. An open house should always happen the first weekend when listed if possible.

Now that you have made your house accessible to view, what should you expect from the real estate agent?

AGENT DIDN'T GO
ABOVE & BEYOND
CHAPTER 14

"I find that the harder I work, the more luck I seem to have." —THOMAS JEFFERSON

You need to hire an agent that goes above and beyond and follows a system with the most aggressive marketing to sell houses. An agent that is readily available and willing to do what needs to be done to sell your house (within the law and ethically). I will give you some examples of how I have helped my clients above and beyond and was more than happy to do it! The next agent you hire should be able to provide you at least a couple examples when you ask the question "How have you gone above and beyond for a client?" The agent you interview should be thrilled to share at least one story because this business is about helping people.

Hardwood Floors Gone Bad

I was helping a family sell a house that they inherited which was a nice house and pretty much move in ready. The family made it very clear to me that they were going to sell the house as-is because they did not want to spend time and money doing repairs to the house. Since they lived over an hour away from the house, I agreed that selling as-is would be the best strategy. I gave them some advice of things to do to get top dollar for the house which included cleaning everything out of the house since everything was outdated. The house also had a musty smell coming from the carpeting. I pulled up the corners of the carpeting in the living room and dining room to see if there was hardwood underneath and sure enough, the hardwood flooring underneath was well preserved (so I thought). Because of the musty carpet smell, I recommended that they remove it and showcase the hardwood flooring.

After my clients removed all the furniture from the house, they removed the musty carpeting. The problem was, once they did that, there were areas with unfinished plywood.

Pictured above: Plywood and stains in flooring did not look good

This was not going to sell the house for top dollar because it did not look good. First impressions are everything to a buyer and seeing these areas of unfinished plywood would turn buyers off. My clients made it very clear that they did not want to spend any money doing repairs or upgrades when we had our first initial meeting so I paid my carpet guy to come in and install new carpet at no cost to the seller. Did the seller ask me to install carpeting? The answer is no. I came to the house after they cleaned out the house and I didn't like the way it looked so I paid for the work to get done. I went above and beyond what was required because protecting my clients bottom line is very important even if it affects mine. By paying for the carpeting, it allowed us to get multiple offers and sell the house for more than list price and for more than the seller thought was possible.

Pictured above: Same photo from last page with virtual staging and carpet

Spot the Cat

Spot, the beloved pet of one of my clients, Charles, ran away during the move when we sold his house. Charles was distraught because winter was right around the corner and feared the cat would not survive the cold weather. It was heartbreaking for him and for me to see him worried. I have pets so I know how a pet is a member of the family and can be very devastating if a pet is lost. The worst part about the situation was that he moved to another state so it was impossible for him to catch Spot. I did not live in the neighborhood either so I knew this would not be an easy thing to do. The cat was also very fearful of humans when it was in the outside environment, so it was not like anyone could go up to the cat and pick her up.

So I did what anyone else would do when they have a lost pet. My team and I put up hundreds of flyers throughout the neighborhood and surrounding neighborhoods offering a $500 reward for Spot's capture. I figured this perhaps would motivate younger kids to help since $500 is a lot of money to someone in middle or high school. We also went door to door and talked to people about Spot and the reward we were offering. We also sent out over 2,000 mailers with Spot's picture and the information for the reward with my personal cell phone.

Every couple days I would get a call from someone with a lead on Spot. Unfortunately, many people were not comfortable with putting out food every day because they either had dogs and were scared the dog would go into the trap or they were worried about the food attracting coyotes (coyotes were seen from time to time here). One neighbor introduced me to a lady in the area that volunteered for the cat shelter. She told me that she had traps that were specifically designed to catch cats that would not harm the cat. She even showed me how to use the trap and set it up. She informed me that we had to put food out in the morning and take it down before dark because it might attract coyotes, racoons, possums, skunks, and other nocturnal animals. This meant that whoever we got to volunteer to help us would have to do a lot of work each day (set up the trap in the morning, put the food in the trap, take the food out of the trap at night, and close the trap at night).

One of the calls came from a good Samaritan by the name of Judy which turned into a great lead. She thought that Spot would come into her back yard but wasn't sure it was the right cat. She described Spot in detail and sure enough, the description fit the bill. Since we had a really good lead, she put food out every day to attract Spot. For the first few days Spot would only eat the food outside the trap. Eventually Spot became more comfortable with the trap and would eat further and further in the trap. Just as Spot was becoming very comfortable with the trap Judy had a trip planned to visit some friends in Michigan so she would not be able to put out the food every day and take the trap down at night. I did not want to disturb Spots daily habit of coming around the house for food so I had one of my assistants go every morning to set up, go during the day to check on things, and go at night to take it down. Spot even started becoming comfortable with my assistant being there.

Pictured above: Photo my assistant took of Spot in the back yard while putting food out each day.

After a few days of putting food out, we caught Spot. We immediately loaded Spot into my car, started driving towards Wisconsin, and called Charles. We met Charles at a motel in Wisconsin and he was thrilled to see her. He never thought he was going to see her again, so he was ecstatic. His wife was also overjoyed and almost in disbelief we caught Spot.

Visit www.joshuainglis.com/testimonial and to see how happy Charles was to see Spot.

Note: The $500 reward was donated to charity. I gave the reward to Judy since we would not have been able to catch Spot without her help and she donated all of the money to the Leukemia & Lymphoma Society which is a wonderful cause. Visit www.lls.org to learn more and donate.

Financial Difficulties

I wish that 100% of my transactions went smoothly, but I would be lying if I said every transaction did. There are things that will happen outside of your control even with the best systems and procedures. This is a story of a transaction that went sideways.

My team and I listed a house for one of my clients who had a very bad experience with her previous real estate agent. The previous agent actually made her cry by some of the things he had said to her and was very unprofessional. The previous agent belittled her and made it seem that he was doing her a favor by being her real estate agent. Under no circumstances should this ever happen, but it did, and the sellers were under a lot of stress after this experience.

The sellers were having financial difficulties and the house needed some updates in order to sell for a good price. I had granite countertops installed in the kitchen and bathroom to update the house. I also had brand new stainless-steel appliances installed in the kitchen. The owners did not have the capacity to pay for these upgrades so I paid for them out of pocket and the plan was to get reimbursed after closing. We then raised the purchase price and received an offer on the house a few weeks later for more than their previous list price! The sellers were ecstatic. I called the buyer's loan officer and interviewed them before we accepted the contract. The buyer's loan officer told me that he wished all of his clients were as good as this buyer and it would be a very smooth closing.

Fast forward 45 days, just a few days away from closing, my clients had made plans to move to Florida. I spoke to the loan officer as my clients were in the process of moving and the loan officer assured me that there was nothing to worry about and we would close as promised. On the day of closing, we found out the buyers couldn't get approved! My attorney and I both spoke to the loan officer several times before the closing day and were lied to the entire time. This put my clients in a very difficult position. The move to Florida included using some of the money from closing to pay for their rent. Since there was no closing, there was no way to pay for the rent.

This made me sick to my stomach because my clients were in a worse situation than before. At least before they had a place to live. For that reason, I paid their first month's rent as a gift and gave them a loan for a few thousand dollars to pay me back if and when the house sold.

At this point I had over $10,000 in this house between upgrades in the house, gifts, and loans, not to mention the few thousand dollars I had in marketing expenses (everything I talk about in this book, professional photos, virtual staging, high def video, 3d tour, drone, mailers, etc.).

We had to relist the house but unfortunately the market had begun to soften. The owners had the water turned off on the day of closing because they thought the house was going to be sold. You do not want to sell a house if the water doesn't work because buyers will associate it with a foreclosure. For this reason, I told my client we needed to get the water turned back on. The water company gave her a window of 8am to 4pm to turn the water back on and told her someone had to be there. She of course could not meet them because she lived in Florida. I volunteered to wait at the house because this was the only way we would be able to sell the house for top dollar. I arrived very early in the morning just in case they came early and the water guy did not arrive until a few minutes before 4pm (funny how that happens most of the time).

While I was at the house I noticed that it did not show well vacant at all. We had a lot of showings when we were on the market previously and had a lot of negative feedback about the pink and blue tiles, the light fixtures, and the condition of the carpeting on the main level. For this reason, I hired a few different contractors to replace the carpeting and tile on the main level as well as replace the light fixtures. The paint for the two-story wall in the great room and office looked bad after they removed pictures and wall hangings so I had them sanded, patched, and repainted. I then had to get the house professionally cleaned because doing work can create a mess. I spent several more thousand dollars to get the house to where it needed to be and never asked the homeowner for a dime for the work we did after the buyers backed out. Why? Because it was the right thing to do. My client was not in a position to do the work or pay for it so I had to roll up my sleeves, get dirty, and open up my wallet again.

After I did all the work on the house the original buyers worked with a better loan officer and were able to close a few weeks later. I wanted to be ready in case the loan did not work out and even though this closed, I still lost money because the commission did not cover all the expenses I incurred. Why would I pay for all of this work and actually lose money to sell a house? It is because I believe in going above and beyond and doing the right thing. This business is much more than making a living, its doing the right thing and helping people when they are in a time of need. Jonathan Lister says it best "As marketers we should be changing the mantra from always be closing to always be helping".

The Typical Agents Marketing Plan

If you read chapters 1 – 13 you know that I utilize very aggressive marketing to help sell my clients houses for top dollar. To get a condensed version of the marketing plan I use, instead of rereading this entire book, visit www.joshuainglis.com/marketing

Here is what many real estate agents will do to market a house:

1. Take pictures with a camera phone
2. Put the property on the MLS

1. Take pictures with a camera phone

Many agents will just use their camera phone to take photos of your house to save time, money, and hassle. Although camera phones have gotten substantially better in quality over the years, it still does not compare with photos taken by a professional photographer. Even five dollar items listed for sale on Ebay have better photos than many of the houses I see listed with other real estate agents. It is really sad that the majority of agents do not hire professional photographers to take photos because a house is one of the biggest investments that a person makes.

2. Put the property on the MLS

Many agents will tell you how great their brokerage is and will rely on the name brand of their office. They will tell you that their brokerage sells lots of houses in the area and that the brokerage has the best marketing plan out there to sell your house for top dollar. They will also tell you about all of the websites your house will go on and how you will get exposure all over the internet with their offices cutting edge technology. What this really means is that they will slap your house on the MLS which is what every other real estate agent will do for you. They then rely on the MLS to do all the work and sell your house.

So What is the MLS?

MLS stands for Multiple Listing Service, which is a tool that real estate agents use to list houses for sale and market them. You must be a real estate agent to post a property to the MLS and you also must be a member of the MLS by paying fees for it. It helps listing agents find cooperative agents that are working with a buyer to sell a house. Vice versa, it helps agents that are working with buyers to find houses for them that are available for sale. The MLS also gives agents information on what commission/co-op fee is being offered by the seller if their client purchases the house.

Agents can run reports and use different tools within the MLS for analyzing market data. Limited access is given to people in the public for free if they are working with a real estate agent and full access is only given to real estate agents that are members of the MLS.

An agent can set up automatic searches for houses that meet certain criteria to send to a client several times a day and the agent does not even need to login to the system.

The MLS is the number one crutch that real estate agents rely on to do all the work. The MLS syndicates a single listing to thousands of websites which include Zillow, Trulia, Realtor.com, and Redfin. If a house doesn't sell, many agents will blame the house, the seller, or the price. Many agents take the approach that once the house is in the MLS, the agents job to market the house is over. My marketing philosophy is that once the house is listed in the MLS, my job to market the property has just begun!

THE IDEAL REAL ESTATE AGENT

If you want to sell your house instead of just listing it, you need to hire the ideal real estate agent. The ideal real estate agent possesses certain qualities that you should look for.

Responsive

An agent and their team should be available to answer questions that a client has outside of regular working hours. That is why being a real estate agent is not a Monday through Friday 9am to 5pm job or a part-time endeavor. The agent and their team must be able to accommodate showing requests from other agents and clients at the drop of a dime to ensure that a ready and able buyer does not slip through their fingers and purchase another home.

A buyer that purchased one of my listings in one day after going live, had another offer on a house and had to make a decision by the following day by 5pm. If someone my team or myself was unable to show the buyer my listing the day he called, he would have likely purchased the other house and we would have lost our buyer. The average days on market for a house of that size in that town was 517 days (According to data from MRED-Midwest Real Estate Data) and I sold that house in one day. The previous agent was unable to sell the house and yet I was able to sell it one day? How is that even possible? Simple, responsiveness. If I did not show this buyer the house with only a few hours notice, we could have lost our buyer and might not have been able to sell it right away. It could have taken the average days on market of 517 days to sell if I didn't meet the buyer there on the day we listed it. Remember, it only takes one person to purchase a house and is why every showing is important. You do not want a buyer to ever fall through the cracks because an agent is unable to accommodate a showing request and is not responsive.

Visit www.solditinaday.com to read more about this story.

Hardworking

You want an agent that believes in hard work and an agent that will work hard for you. Unfortunately, hard work is not a skill that is easily taught. One of my favorite quotes is by Thomas Edison "Opportunity is missed by most people because it is dressed in overalls and looks like work." No one has ever become a self-made millionaire by sleeping in every day and watching tv for 4 hours a day.

Hard work is probably something that is my DNA. When I was in high school I had two part-time jobs while playing basketball, running cross country, and running track. When I went to college full time with over 20 credit hours each semester, I also worked a full-time job from 11pm to 7am five days a week. I would work overnight, get four hours of sleep, and then drive to school which was 30 minutes to an hour away depending on traffic. I will never stop working hard because I believe hard work is essential to being successful at anything in life. The harder you work, the luckier you get. Make sure the agent you hire works hard for you!

A Learner

A question you should ask any agent that you interview is "How much money have you spent on your real estate education?" The truth is, many agents will study to get their real estate license and then rarely go to any classes after that.

If they do go to classes or events to learn, it is typically the events that the office puts on where there is a free lunch.

I have spent over $100,000 on my real estate and business education (outside of college). I do not say that to impress you or shock you, I say that to simply illustrate that I believe that a person should never stop learning. I did not invent the strategies in this book, I learned about them, tweaked them, and implemented them into my business. I will always invest in the biggest asset I own, my brain.

Many agents live by the motto ABC – Always Be Closing

I live by the motto ABL – Always Be Learning

An Implementer

Pablo Picasso said, "Action is the foundational key to all success." You can have all the knowledge in the world but if you do not implement that knowledge, it does not make a difference. You want to hire an agent that continually educates him/herself and someone that implements the strategies that he/she learns.

You can easily tell if an agent is an implementer if they are using 3d virtual tours, video, and drone photography on their listings. Those types of marketing are cutting edge and are well known by most real estate agents, the question is how many agents are implementing it into their marketing?

Systematic

Good systems and checklists need to be in place to sell your house quickly for top dollar. An agent that goes wherever the wind takes them is not going to properly market your house for sale. As an example, pilots follow checklists for preflight, engine start, after engine start, before takeoff, after takeoff, climb, decent, before landing, after landing, shutdown, etc. Pilots that have done their jobs for 20+ years and flown thousands of flights, still use checklists even though they can probably do the checklists in their sleep. The real estate agent you hire to sell your house should do the same so nothing is missed.

Ask the agent you interview for the marketing checklist that they follow to sell a house. To see my marketing checklist visit www.joshuainglis.com/marketing/

An Investor

You want an agent that invests in your success and invests money to sell your house. If an agent invests money in marketing to sell your house with professional photos, video, 3d, mailers, drone, facebook ads, etc. they are financially vested to sell your house. The real estate agent should only get reimbursed for the marketing if the house sells which means the agent will work hard until it sells. Some agents will try to spend as little money as possible to market a house in case it does not sell. This is so there is little to no financial risk on the real estate agent's part. A general rule of thumb is the agent should be spending 0.5% – 1% of your sales price to market your house. If your house value is $100,000 the agent should be spending a minimum of $500 to market your house.

The agent should always foot the bill for the marketing that is created for the house unless the real estate agent gives the homeowner a valuation and the homeowner still wants to list the house at a number that is not realistic. I don't expect any agent to cover the bill to market a house that is unrealistically priced by a seller which leads into the next quality.

A Straight Shooter

You want an agent that tells you the truth, even if it hurts. I always provide feedback from other agents and buyers whether it is good, bad, or ugly. An agent that tries to sugar coat everything is not going to be effective at selling your house. You are an adult and should be treated that way even when there is bad news. Being a real estate agent is like being a doctor. Imagine if a doctor knows that you have a life-threatening illness but doesn't tell you the news and pretends like everything is ok. This illness could have been cured easily if action was taken early, but the longer you have the illness, the more life threatening it becomes and the more difficult it becomes to cure. This doctor would probably be sued for medical malpractice and would lose his/her license. This scenario with the doctor sounds crazy to even think about, but a similar scenario happens with real estate agents all the time.

I see people that will list a house with an agent simply because that agent said they can sell it at a price that is not realistic. The homeowner then becomes a victim of a listing agreement and is locked into a contract. The owner will then have to decide if they should continue to let the house sit on the market for months without selling, or if they should do price drops until it finally sells for less than its real value because it accumulated so much market time. Once a house accumulates a high number of days on market, it will typically sell for much less than the home that was priced right from the beginning. If an offer is made by someone, the buyer will typically be in control of the selling process because over months of sitting on the market, the seller becomes desperate and the seller has lost any leverage they might have. The buyer knows that if they walk after they put the house under contract, the seller will be in an even worse position, so the buyer and the buyer's agent will use that as leverage.

Which doctor would you prefer: the one that lies to you even when you have a life-threatening illness or the one that tells you how it is so you can immediately take action to cure the disease? Think about the next real estate agent that you hire the same way and you will always make the right choice.

Lives by the Golden Rule

You want an agent that lives by the golden rule. Someone that treats others the way they want to be treated. This business is not about houses, it is about people. As a real estate agent, I help people go through one of the biggest transitions in life and I treat it with the respect it deserves. Zig Ziglar said "You can get everything in life you want if you will just help enough other people get what they want." When I deliver far more value than I charge, it creates lasting relationships beyond the house and a one time transaction. If someone doesn't think of me the next time they need the services of a real estate agent or they don't recommend me to their friends and family, I failed. That means I did not provide service that was above and beyond. After someone works with me, I want to be the only logical choice! The next agent you hire should feel the same way.

In Summary

Going above and beyond is imperative to sell your house for top dollar. If real estate is Monday through Friday 9am to 5pm or a part time endeavor for an agent, they are probably not the agent you want to hire. Your house is one of the largest investments you make and you need to hire someone who is willing to do whatever it takes to get the job done (ethically and legally). Look for an agent that is willing to go the extra mile and is willing to follow the steps outlined in this book because an agent that follows the steps in this book is already going above and beyond. You want an agent that is responsive, hardworking, a learner, an implementer, systematic, invests in your success, a straight shooter, and lives by the golden rule. Anything less than that and you are selling yourself and your house short.

Now that you have a Rockstar real estate agent that will go above and beyond for you, what price should you list the house at?

YOUR HOUSE IS
OVERPRICED

CHAPTER 15

"Nothing is more expensive than a missed opportunity." —H. JACKSON BROWN, JR

You have to price your house strategically using the recently sold houses in your neighborhood as a guide and use the market research we talked about in Chapter 1. Houses that are priced right from the get go will sell for more than a house that is overpriced from the beginning because the house will get caught in a dangerous price drop spiral. The longer your house is on the market, the less it will ultimately sell for. Potential buyers will begin to wonder why your house has been listed for a long time and begin to form theories like there must be something wrong with the house. Another theory buyers and agents will form is that the seller must be desperate at this point because it has been listed for a long time. This will open your house to low ball offers which are below your houses true market value.

In 2013, McEarney Associates, a McLean VA real estate company, found that houses that went under contract the first week they were listed, sold for an average of 2.08 percentage above list price. Houses that were on the market for 4 months sold for an average of 11.53 percent below their original price.

I have seen the same thing in my market. Houses that are priced right from the beginning will sell for more than other houses in the neighborhood. I will give you an example, I listed a house for $450,000 in a neighborhood where most agents listed houses at $499,000. After several price drops and several months later, the houses would sell very close to $450,000. We did the opposite, we priced the house at $450,000 right from the very beginning. We received 9 offers and sold the house AS-IS and over $20,000 over asking setting a new record in the neighborhood for the highest sales price! Keep in mind, this house needed new flooring on the entire first floor and new windows too. But because we priced the house correctly from the beginning the seller was in complete control at all times. The seller had all of the negotiation power because if we didn't come to an agreement with an offer, we had 8 other offers waiting. That was how we were able to negotiate an AS-IS offer and chose the strongest offer which we were able to close in 3 weeks.

Also keep in mind, when you overprice a house, you will actually help your competition sell faster. Potential buyers will compare your smaller house with less amenities to a bigger house with more amenities or updates. When someone goes to a house that is overpriced and then goes to a house that is priced right, the thought process for the person at the house that is priced right will be something like "Wow, this house is much nicer than the last house we just saw, this house is a bargain!"

As a general rule of thumb, for every 10 showings you receive on your house, you should get at least one offer or you are asking too much for your house.

If your house was listed for a year, how many showings did you receive during that time frame? If the answer is 20-30 without one offer, you were probably overpriced because you should have received 2-3 offers during that time frame. If you were not receiving at least one showing a week, you were likely overpriced. If you received 0 to 5 showings over a one-year time frame you are likely drastically over-priced.

Appraisals

Houses do not always sell for what they are worth, they sell for what a buyer and seller agree upon and what they will appraise for. Even if you manage to convince a buyer to pay more for your house than other houses in the area, you will likely have an issue with the appraisal. The appraiser is going to use recently sold data from the last 6 months in your neighborhood. Unless your house is bigger than all of the other houses in your neighborhood, you are likely going to have an issue with your house appraising. Even if your house is more updated than the other houses, it will likely not appraise for the contract price that the buyer agreed to pay. Appraisers for banks are different from the appraisers you independently hire. The appraiser for the bank is representing the banks interest, not yours. The banks appraiser is making sure that the value that the buyer is paying is in line with everything else in the neighborhood so if they have to take the property back, they are not upside down. The bank does not make risky loans and loaning money for an overpriced asset is extremely risky. Let's use an example of a new car. If a dealership has two identical models for sale and someone really wants to buy that model and can purchase one of them for $35,000 and the other one for $40,000, which one would someone purchase? If they are truly identical, everyone would purchase the $35,000 car. The bank uses the same logic and will not fund a house for $400,000 if they believe it is only worth $350,000.

So what happens if the appraisal comes in lower than the agreed upon price between the buyer and seller? There are 4 things that you can do as a seller:

1. Contest the Appraisal

You can contest the appraisal but you are likely only going to get one shot at it. You will have to provide data on why the appraisal was low. If you do not have data for houses that sold at the contract price or for more that are the same square footage or smaller than your house, you are beating a dead horse. The bank is simply going to be looking at a cost per square foot and what has sold. If there is no recently sold data at the contract price within 6 months within a half mile, it does not matter. The bank is not going to budge and won't fund the loan for the buyer.

What is even worse is when the buyer's loan was FHA, the appraisal will stick with the property for 6 months! That means that if a different buyer comes along with FHA financing, the old appraisal will still be used by the new bank.

2. Have the Buyer Bring Cash for the Difference

You can require that the buyer has to come up with the difference between the appraised value and the contract price in cash. The problem with that is a buyer must have the ability to bring extra money to the table that cannot be financed. Many times, a buyer has a certain amount of money dedicated toward the down payment, now they have to come up with more cash out of their pocket. It is not a good feeling for a buyer to have to cough up more cash.

Keep in mind a buyer does not like to feel like they are getting a bad deal either. It can make a person feel foolish and no one likes to be made a fool of for someone else's personal gain. If the bank says the house is worth X, why should I pay Y?

It is very rare that a buyer will bring the cash for the full amount between the appraised value and the contract price. What commonly happens is the seller will lower their price to the appraised value or the buyer and seller will split the difference between the appraisal and contract price. For example, if the house appraised for $700,000 but the contract price was $750,000 and the seller and buyer agree to split the difference between the appraisal and contract price, the buyer will bring the $25,000 difference to the table in cash.

Since a buyer does not want to feel like they are getting a bad deal, many times a buyer will just walk unless the owner drops their price to the appraised value of $700,000 in the previous example.

3. Finance the deal for the new buyer

What if I just finance the difference between the appraised value and the contract price? Unfortunately, the bank will not allow a second lien or an outside loan to be put on title when it closes. You, the seller, would have to finance the entire amount of the loan or a large portion of it. This is called seller financing. The biggest issue with this strategy is that if you have a loan on your property now, it will need to be paid off first before you can finance someone else to buy your house. I go into this strategy at the end of this chapter if you want to learn how to sell your house for more than its market value if your house is paid off.

4. <u>Kill the deal and relist the house</u>

You can always kill the deal if the buyer does not come up with the difference in cash for the appraised value vs the contract price. The problem then becomes that you reactivate your house to the marketplace and give new buyers the upper hand in negotiations. One of the first questions potential buyers will ask is why did the house get reactivated? Many times buyers will just assume that there may be something wrong with the house and is the reason why the house didn't close after going under contract. Once a house goes under contract and gets reactivated, the house will sell for less money the second time around typically. The reason for this is because the house is no longer new and potential buyers put a stigma on the house for falling out of contract. That is why it is important to price the house correctly right from the very beginning.

HOW MUCH IS MY HOUSE WORTH?

Before you ever list your house, it is important to know what it is worth. Many people think that they should contact an appraiser and pay them hundreds of dollars to find out how much a property is worth but there is another way. If you are looking for a way to find out the value of your house and do not want to pay for an appraisal, you should contact a real estate agent who understands complex valuation.

If the buyer has more information than the seller, the buyer typically has the upper hand in negotiations and will buy the house for less than what it is worth. If the seller has the same or more information than the buyer, they will be able to sell the house for its actual value.

You will want to make sure the appraiser or agent that does the home valuation takes the following things into consideration when valuating your house:

• Have the sold properties closed within the last 3 months, 6 months, or 12 months?

• Are the recently sold properties within the same neighborhood? (Example: a subdivision built in the 2000's may be next to a subdivision built in the 1970's)

• Are the recently sold properties within a half mile? (If you are in a city environment like Chicago, you may only be able to use recently sold properties within the same block or street. If in a rural environment, you can go out a mile or further in some cases)

• Is the square footage for the recently sold properties within 5 percent of each other? (Basement square footage does not count the same as living space above ground)

• Do the recently sold properties have the same grade school, middle school, and high school?

• Are you only looking at recently sold properties or are you looking at active properties on the market? (Just because something in the neighborhood is listed actively for $50,000 higher than everyone else does not mean they will get it)

- Are the recently sold properties the same model with similar amenities? (Example: a two-story house with a basement and a raised ranch are completely different)
- Do the recently sold properties have similar lots or do they have much larger lots. In Chicago, you cannot compare a property on a double lot to a property on a standard 25x125 lot
- Is your house on a busy street? (Houses on busy streets can easily be 10-30% lower in value compared to houses in a subdivision)
- Are the recently sold properties on the other side of a busy street or railroad tracks? (Busy streets are typically a dividing line because those houses are in a different neighborhood. Ever hear the expression wrong side of the tracks? That is because usually neighborhoods on one side of a railroad track are much different than the neighborhood on the other side.)
- Do the recently sold properties have the same number of garage spaces? (Also look at detached vs attached)
- Do the recently sold properties have updated heating and central air?
- Do the recently sold properties have updated electrical and plumbing?
- Are the recently sold properties brick houses or are they frame? This makes a big difference in Chicago.
- What year were the kitchen and bathrooms updated? (Extreme example: If the kitchen was replaced only 8 years ago in the Lincoln Park neighborhood of Chicago, it is considered an outdated kitchen and will likely sell for hundreds of thousands dollars less than a recent remodel with modern wall colors)

- What kind of flooring do the recently sold properties have? (if your house has carpet on the second floor and all of the other properties have hardwood floors, this will affect your resale value)
- Do the recently sold properties have similar views? (High vantage point, views of the downtown area, views of the water, and views of nature all affect property value)
- Does your house or any of the recently sold properties back up to a warehouse, busy street, train tracks, or power lines?
- Are any of the recently sold properties closer to the downtown area? Usually the closer, the higher the value.

These are just a few of the things you need to consider when evaluating a house. It is very easy to see how sites like Zillow, Trulia, or the tax assessor can be less than accurate. That is why you should contact a real estate agent who understands complex property valuation.

If you live in Chicago or the suburbs of Chicago, my team can do a free home valuation on your house. Visit www.chicagoandburbs.com *for a free home valuation.*

Information is Not Enough

Even if a seller has all the information in the world but doesn't have an aggressive agent, it will not matter.

Michael, a member of a church congregation, contacted me after I helped sell his house that backed up to the rail road tracks when the two previous agents could not. He figured if I could help him sell his house where others failed, I could also help his congregation buy a property. The seller of the building they wanted to purchase spent over $2,000 on a commercial appraisal that was 157 pages a few weeks before Michael contacted me. The appraisal came in at $950,000 which was what the seller wanted, Michael and the congregation were devastated.

Michael and the church committee could not pay that kind of money for the building because they were a very small congregation. I had pretty intense negotiations between myself and the other real estate agent. Long story short, I was able to negotiate the seller and other agent down to $540,000 which was a price the congregation could afford which was almost half of the appraised value! Of course, I did not do this on my own, I had the entire church praying for me and divine intervention. This is why having all the information AND having an aggressive real estate agent working for you are equally important. Even when a seller spent over two thousand dollars on a very detailed appraisal and had 157 pages of data, it did not matter when an aggressive agent like myself was involved on the other side.

What to Do if Your House is Upside Down

Your house might be overpriced simply because you owe more than what it is worth. This is commonly referred to as being upside down. This is a tough situation for most and can be very discouraging for anyone. This can make a person sick to their stomach and make them lose sleep at night worrying about what can be done. I know this feeling because I have been upside down with several of my properties. Everyone that purchased real estate in 2006 and 2007 know exactly what I am talking about. Everyone thought they had a house that was worth one number and just a few years later it was worth half of it's value at the peak. If you are upside down and do not have any hope, remember the words of Sir Winston Churchill "Never give in, never give in, never, never, never-in nothing, great or small, large or petty."

There are always options you can pursue if you take action right away. Take action wisely though because there are a lot of companies and even some attorneys that try to take advantage of the situation when people are in trouble. If you are upside down, you never want to pay a large upfront fee to anyone. I recommend you only hire a company that is vested in your success and only gets paid after the service is completed. Never pay a company instead of paying your mortgage, I have seen dozens of people fall into this trap. The people end up in a bigger hole than they were to begin with.

Note: If you do ever pay a company anything upfront, make sure they have a brick and mortar business in the state you live in that you can visit. Many companies that are scamming people do not even do business in the state they are located in. The reason for this is because it takes longer for the Federal Government to investigate a company that is scamming people than the State Government if a business crosses state lines. Once the Federal Government investigates a company or shuts them down, they start another company in another state with a different name and do the same thing over again.

Every situation is different but many times a person can do what's called a short sale. A short sale is when the house is sold for less than the current mortgage balance and the owner of the house does not have to bring the difference in cash to sell the house (the bank takes a loss). A short sale is great because it allows the owner to sell their house for less than what is owed. Many times, the seller will even get relocation assistance or money from the bank. I have seen relocation assistance money over $15,000 and the sellers were upside down on their house. There is no guarantee that relocation assistance will be given to a seller that is upside down, but it is much more common that a seller will get some relocation assistance money than not.

A short sale is a great option for a seller that is upside down because it does not cost the homeowner anything! The agent involved only gets paid if the short sale is successful and the agent actually gets paid by the bank. If a company or real estate agent tries to charge for short sale services, find another company or agent. If there is an attorney involved, they should also only get paid if the short sale closes and is successful.

In order for a seller to qualify for a short sale, the seller will need to have some sort of hardship. Those hardships can be everything from reduced hours at work, relocation or future relocation, reduced income, a death in the family, divorce, medical issues, and various other reasons. The bank will want a hardship letter and I recommend that someone who can really explain what happened write it, preferably a woman. Men typically do not explain things in the same detail that a woman will (sorry guys). I always tell people the goal of the hardship letter should be to make the person reading the letter cry. The letter should be handwritten and explain why the seller is in the situation that they are in. The bank will also look at the seller's tax returns, bank statements, w2's, etc.

You only want to work with an agent who has short sale experience or an agent that has a team to negotiate the short sale. I have always used a team to negotiate short sales because it is a full-time job. The short sale negotiators I work with have relationships with asset managers at each of the banks/lending institutions and know how to properly submit a short sale package. This ensures the short sale package we submit stays at the top of the pile. Anyone that submits an incomplete short sale package or improper short sale package goes to the bottom of the pile and decreases the likelihood of a successful closing. Every lender's short sale package is a little bit different and that is why it is important to work with someone that has worked with your particular lender. I cannot keep up with every new nuance that US Bank or Citi Mortgage changes, so I use a team to negotiate my short sale listings who stay up to date with all of the lender processes.

Short Sale Credit Myth

You might be thinking to yourself, "What about my credit!? It's going to be ruined! The biggest myth about short sales is that it will devastate a person's credit. This is simply not true. Many short sales that I have been involved in showed that the loan was fully satisfied which did not impact the seller's credit one point. What impacts a seller's credit score the most is the missed payments to the bank. Many banks are even allowing short sales to occur when a borrower is current on their mortgage payments, which means a short sale might not even affect a borrower's credit at all!

I have good news for your credit even if you have missed payments or are behind on payments. You can increase your credit score very quickly with this one trick I am going to share. This trick is worth at least 100 times more than whatever price you paid for this book if you have a challenged credit score. To increase your credit score very quickly after you go through a rough patch (not just a short sale), open a credit card account if all of your credit card accounts have been closed. If you open a credit card and have bad credit, that's ok, even if they give you an extremely low limit. With this new or existing credit card, you will want to make daily

payments to the credit card. You read that right, DAILY!
Make a payment for $5, $10, $20, it doesn't matter.
Download the credit card company's app for your smart
phone and link it to your bank account. This makes
payments quick, easy, and painless. You will always want to
keep a very small balance on the credit card less than 35% of
the total limit. Never pay off the credit card balance or this
trick is not as effective.

If you make 365 payments to a credit card company in a
year, it is treated almost as if you have made over 30 years of
on time payments! How is that possible you are probably
thinking to yourself!? The reason is because most people pay
monthly, which the credit card company receives 12
payments in a year typically. By paying daily, take 365 and
divide it by 12. That comes out to 30.4166666667. As you
can see, any person with an equivalent of 30 years of on time
credit card payments is credit worthy!

How to Sell Your House for More Than Fair Market Value

You might have purchased this book simply because you
wanted to know how to sell a house for more than its market
value after reading the back of this book. You might not want
to lower your asking price for your house even if you received
feedback from ten or more people that you are overpriced.
You might not even care that there aren't any houses in your
neighborhood that have sold for what you are asking. I don't

blame you, everyone wants top dollar for their house so that is why this section was written for you.

The secret to selling your house for more than what it is worth is advertising that you are willing to do seller financing. What is seller financing? Seller financing is acting like the bank for the buyer. Instead of a buyer getting a loan to purchase your house from the bank, the buyer gets a loan from you to purchase the house. This means that you must have your house paid off or have a very small loan that you can pay off when you sell it. You cannot use this strategy if you are not in a place to pay off a mortgage balance. You want to advertise the home as follows in the description in the very first line: NO BANKS NEEDED, SELLER FINANCING AVAILABLE!

I suggest getting a down payment of at least 5% of the purchase price. For example: if you are selling your home for one million dollars, you should require that the buyer put $50,000 as a down payment minimum. If you are selling a house for $200,000 the buyer needs to put at least $10,000 down.

I have even sold some of my own houses for well over market value using this strategy because people will pay a premium for seller financing.

What type of people does seller financing attract? The answer is all types of people, let's dive into who exactly seller financing attracts and why people are willing to pay a premium.

Foreign Nationals: It is difficult for foreign nationals to get loans in the United States even if they are very wealthy and make great money. There are also several laws that only allow foreign nationals to transfer a certain amount of money into the United States every year. This means that even if a foreign national has one hundred million dollars in a bank account overseas, it will take a very long time to transfer all of that money into the United States. This means that foreign nationals are very limited in what they can and can't purchase. Seller financing bridges the gap for someone that has just started the process for moving money into the United States. Now a foreign national can own a home instead of renting and they will pay a premium for this. Foreign nationals are typically interested in seller financing for middle to higher end houses.

Investors: Most people think that investors pay less than market value for houses and this is typically true unless a seller is willing to finance them. The investor has to be able to make money somehow so the numbers have to make sense one way or another. If the investor is paying more than market value, they typically have to make some sort of cash flow from renting out the house. Investors that purchase houses with seller financing are usually looking at a long play. I work with a lot of investors and every time I mention the words seller financing to one, an angel gets its wings. Investors are typically interested in seller financing for low to middle priced houses because typically the rent will not cover the mortgage payment for luxury houses.

People with a Bankruptcy, Short Sale, or Foreclosure: Just because someone has a bankruptcy, short sale, or foreclosure in their past, does not make them a bad borrower necessarily. Sometimes it was something as simple as being laid off for two years and now they have a job making twice what they were making before. There are restrictions on how long after a bankruptcy, short sale, or foreclosure that someone can get a traditional loan on a home again. Many times people in these situations have saved up a sizeable amount for a down payment (I've seen where people buy a house for cash one year after a foreclosure!). If this person can prove they are making a good income they might be an ideal candidate for seller financing. I would recommend that you require at least fifteen percent down from someone in this situation to protect yourself. People with a bankruptcy, short sale, or foreclosure buy homes at all price points.

How to Become the Bank

You need three important things in place to do seller financing to protect yourself as the lender.

Mortgage / Deed of Trust: This is the document that is recorded with the county clerk and recorder to publicly secure your loan against the house. The buyer of the house cannot resell the house without paying off the mortgage first (you).

Promissory Note: This is the borrowers promise to pay you the lender. This outlines the terms of the loan like loan amount, length of loan, frequency of payments, interest rate, etc.

Insurance: You will want to be listed on the borrower's insurance policy as the mortgage holder. This protects you, the lender, against fire, tornadoes, etc. If the borrower cancels the insurance policy, you will be notified.

Since you are not a bank and probably do not want to process a bunch of paperwork, you will probably want to get a mortgage servicer. The servicer keeps track of all the payments, collects payments, holds escrow money, and issues tax documents at the end of the year to the borrower and you the lender. They charge a very nominal fee which is worth it for making your life easier.

You are probably thinking to yourself "But Josh, what if they don't pay me?" Very simple, foreclose and take the asset back. You get to keep the down payment and all payments that the borrower made over the course of the loan. You will also want to get a personal guarantee from the borrower. A personal guarantee allows you to go after someone's assets outside of just the house.

Benefits of Being the Bank

There are several benefits to being the bank and doing seller financing. The biggest benefit is that you are not a landlord, you are the bank and are investing passively. If the buyer's toilet gets clogged, that is not the banks responsibility. I have never heard of anyone calling their bank to unclog a toilet or replace a leaky faucet.

Another big benefit to seller financing for the seller is tax benefits. I'm sure you've heard the expression, "why the rich get richer", this is one of those reasons. Wealthy people understand the tax benefits for passive investing, you do not have to pay capital gains tax on interest payments like you do when you profit from the sale of a property or an investment.

The biggest benefit for seller financing is generational wealth and legacy. Most people want to leave their spouse, kids, and grandkids something when they pass, so this is something that can be handed down. I suggest making a family trust the lender so it can be easily passed down to your loved ones. The family trust continues to get monthly interest payments, even if you are not around any longer.

You can expect to get 4% or more interest annually by offering seller financing. That sure beats 1% sitting in a CD at the bank! The Rule of 72 developed by Albert Einstein states the number of years your investment will take to double, given a fixed annual interest rate. If you sell your house conventionally and put all of that money in a CD at the bank which offers 1% interest, it will take 72 years to double your money! 72 / 1 = 72 years. I don't know about you, but I don't have 72 years to wait around. Let's use a conservative example of a 4% interest rate you charge the borrower with seller financing. 72 / 4 = 18 years. 18 years to double your money sure beats 72 years and 4% is a conservative interest rate to charge. Remember, you are the bank, you can set whatever interest rate and terms you want to charge within reason (not to mention the higher sales price of the house).

As you can see, seller financing is a great strategy to sell your house for more than market value if you are in a position to offer it. Make sure the agent you hire understands seller financing and markets it appropriately so you get the best buyers and borrowers.

In Summary

You can only sell a house for what a buyer and seller will agree to and what it will appraise for unless the buyer brings the difference which is very rare. Pricing a house correctly from the beginning will sell the house for more money than a house that starts at a higher price and drops the price over time.

If you are upside down and owe more than what the house is worth and do not have the ability to bring the difference in equity to closing, you should consider a short sale. Short sales typically do not impact your credit as much as people think and can even put money in a seller's pocket with relocation assistance. You want to make sure the agent you work with has a team to do short sale negotiations with the bank that does not charge an upfront fee.

If your house is paid off and you want to sell your house for more than its worth, you should offer seller financing. You need to have an agent and attorney that understand seller financing so that you are protected and attract the right buyers and borrowers.

Now that you know the 15 reasons why a house doesn't sell, how many reasons apply to your house?

SOLD

NEXT STEPS

CONCLUSION

"The most difficult thing is the decision to act, the rest is merely tenacity." —AMELIA EARHART

Now that you have read the book, which reason or reason(s) is it that your house hasn't sold? Below is the recap of the 15 reasons, put a check next to each reason that is appropriate to your situation.

Was your house strategically priced? If your house was not priced at an even number and was priced at a number like $249,000, $583,120, or $999,999 you were not priced correctly to be optimized in web searches. Almost all searches online happen in even ranges. Did the real estate agent share with you the data on how many buyers were working with agents in the MLS at various price points? If the house was priced at an odd number or if the data for the buyers looking at houses on the MLS was not shared, check the box.

Did you have the best and highest resolution photos taken? Was the front photo an unobstructed view of the front of the house and was the front photo properly landscaped? Did you get aerial photos of the house with a drone and did you get twilight photos taken of the house? If you answered no to any of those questions, check the box.

Did you have a high definition video created for your house? Some people call a virtual tour pictures with piano music but that is a slideshow. A high definition video virtual tour is much different and superior because it is actual video footage. If you have a luxury house, a commercial like video should have been made. Most buyers love watching high quality videos and most people spend 40 minutes a day on YouTube! If professional high definition video was not created for your house, check the box.

Did you have the house professionally staged? Staging does not have to be done physically, it can be done virtually without real furniture. Staging makes empty dull rooms in photos look visually appealing and gives buyers ideas for what can be done to a room. Staged houses typically sell for more than non-staged houses. If the house was not staged professionally either physically or virtually, check the box.

Did the buyers know the layout of the house before they ever scheduled a showing? Were they able to walk through your house virtually with a 3D tour? Your house should have a floorplan created for it like an architect drew them. This increases the number of qualified showings for your house. The house should also have a 3D tour created for it so anyone in the world can virtually walk through the house. The 3D tour allows buyers to make decisions quicker and also keeps buyers engaged longer with your house. If your house did not have floor plans created and a 3D tour, check the box.

Did your house have a custom URL created for it (example www.123mainst.com)? Web appeal is just as important as curb appeal in today's marketplace. You do not want to have to send potential buyers to websites like Zillow or Realtor.com where there are thousands of other competing houses listed for sale. Rather, we want to showcase your house and your house alone on the website with plenty of content which include photos, video, floor plans, 3D tour, etc. If your house did not have a custom website built for it with its own domain name like www.123mainst.com, check the box.

Did your house have professionally printed brochures and marketing materials? Print marketing creates a stronger emotional response for buyers to your house which triggers a greater intent to purchase. It is also something that buyers can take with them so they are reminded of your house at a later date and time if they do not come to a decision right away. If your house did not have professionally printed flyers and business cards created, check the box.

Was your house promoted on the social media platforms: YouTube, Facebook, and LinkedIn? The average person spends 40 minutes a day on YouTube. The video that is uploaded must be properly titled and tagged so it can be found on searches by buyers. The average person spends 35 minutes on Facebook which is a very social site where information about your house is easily shared. A Facebook page should be created for the house and Facebook ads should also be run to promote the house to people in the area. The house should be promoted on LinkedIn with an article and posts since it is the largest B2B platform. The house should also be promoted on other social media platforms but YouTube, Facebook, and LinkedIn are the big 3. If the house was not put on YouTube with proper titling, or if the house did not have its own facebook page with facebook ads, or if the house was not promoted on LinkedIn, check the box.

☐ Did mailings go out to the community with information about your house? 17 times out of 20, the buyer for your house or buyer's friends/family live within a 5mile radius of the house. Direct mail also gets a much higher response rate than other forms of marketing. If mailers did not go out to the community about your house, check the box.

☐ Did the real estate sign in the front yard have multiple ways for a potential buyer to get information about the house? Buyers should be able to get information about your house for sale in different ways when they drive by. They should be able to call the agent, email the agent, visit the website, scan a QR code, or text a 24 hour hotline based on the sign and rider. This increases the likelihood that buyers will raise their hand that they are interested and take the next step for information in a way we want them to receive it. We do not want people to get information about the house on third party websites where thousands of other homes are also for sale. If your house does not have a professional sign with a rider that includes the website and text line, check the box.

☐ Is your house a mess or have too much stuff everywhere? You want to make sure your house is as clean and clutter free as possible. Personal photos should be placed somewhere safe so buyers can envision their family living in the house, not yours. You want to religiously clean your house so that it is almost eat off the floor clean. If you did not remove about 50% of your personal belongings when you listed your house or received feedback that your house was not clean or cramped, check the box.

☐ Did you receive any feedback that your house had an odor? Many buyers will not purchase a house if there is a smoke, animal, cooking, or musty odor. I have worked with clients that loved everything about a house except the smell and did not purchase for that reason. Many buyers are worried that they will not be able to properly remove odors so they don't buy. If you received any feedback from previous showings that your house had an odor, check the box.

☐ Was your house accessible for showings or was it difficult for buyers to view? You want to try to make your house as accessible to potential buyers as possible. Sometimes if a buyer cannot get into a house after a showing request, they may never request to see it again even if the listing agent continues to follow up with the buyer's agent. Many times, buyers will only go out two or three times before deciding. If you turned away two or more showing requests or had limited showing availability, check the box.

☐ Did your agent go above and beyond? A house is one of the largest investments that a person owns and an agent needs to be willing to do whatever it takes (ethically and legally) to sell a house. An agent should be responsive, hardworking, a learner, an implementer, systematic, invests in your success, a straight shooter, and lives by the golden rule. If you do not feel that your agent went above and beyond, check the box.

☐ Did you get feedback that your house was overpriced? As a general rule of thumb, for every 10 showings you should get 1 offer. If you had over 10 showings and did not get an offer, you were likely overpriced. If you were not getting at least one showing a week, you were likely overpriced. A house will only sell for what a buyer and seller will agree on and what a house will appraise for unless the seller finances the buyer to purchase the house. If you weren't getting at least one showing a week or had over ten showings without a single offer, check the box.

So how did your house do? How many boxes did you check that applied to you? See below

1 – 2 boxes checked: This is very easy to fix. You should be able to sell the house relatively easily once adjustments are made by you and your agent.
3 – 4 boxes checked: You and your agent have some work to do but it's nothing that hard work will not fix. If you and your agent strategically address the issues, you will be able to sell the house.
5 – 11 boxes checked: This is concerning. There is a lot of work that will need to be completed to sell your house. You will want to interview new agents that will implement all of the strategies contained in this book if you are not currently listed with an agent. If you have a signed listing agreement with an agent that is active, you need to give this book to your current agent and make sure they address all 15 reasons why your house isn't selling. If the agent refuses to take action, you will want to see when your listing agreement expires. You will also need to take action on the items that you are responsible for if they apply (reasons 11, 12, & 13) which you can do at anytime.
12 – 15 boxes checked: You might need a priest instead of a real estate agent to sell your house. All kidding aside, you have serious problems, it is no wonder why the house didn't sell. You need to do something completely different to sell the house and you may even want to sell it as-is to a real estate investor.

Now that you have reviewed your situation, is it going to be something easy to fix or are you going to do a major overhaul? I hope it is something minor and easy to fix but if it is serious you might need my help.

If You Want My Help and Live in Chicago or in the Suburbs of Chicago

Great news, my team and I will be able to give you a free assessment and help you move forward whether we work together or not.

Note: We do not personally work with everyone and we cannot get involved if your house is currently listed with a real estate agent. If listed, please disregard, this is not a solicitation for listings.

If we are a good fit and decide to work with each other, my team and I will use the strategies contained within this book to sell your house for the most amount of money in the shortest amount of time.

Visit www.chicagoandburbs.com and enter your info for a free home valuation

If You Want a Cash Offer and Live in Chicago or in the Suburbs of Chicago

If your house needs work or TLC and you do not care about getting top dollar, we can give you a cash offer and buy the house as-is in as little as 3 days or on your timeline. Keep in mind with this option that my team or investors would be buying the house as an investment and would need to be able to make a profit. We cannot give you top dollar if you want a cash offer from us or our investors.

Visit www.offerguarantee.com and enter your info for a cash offer

Note: If you want top dollar, you should list your house with a real estate agent that implements ALL of the strategies outlined in this book.

If You Want My Help and Live Outside of the Chicagoland Area

More good news, my team and I will be able to give you a limited assessment. We will be able to connect you with an agent that follows a very aggressive marketing plan very similar to our own that will sell your house for top dollar.

Visit www.fullretailprice.com and enter your info for a free assessment.

What Next?

Take action! Anthony Robbins say's "The path to success is to take massive, determined action". You have the knowledge of what needs to be done, now you need to implement it. You should be able to properly vet any new real estate agents and make sure they follow the blueprint in this book to sell your house. Now it's time for you and your real estate agent to roll up your sleeves and get to work. I wish you the best of luck and look forward to hearing from you and your success story!

Acknowledgments

I am going to keep my acknowledgments short because there have been so many people that have been instrumental to my success that I could write an entire book on this very subject.

I want to start by first and foremost thanking **God** for everything that has been provided to me. Looking back, everything that has happened in my life was for a reason.

I want to thank my father **Bruce Inglis** who was an amazing person that always told me I could become whatever I wanted to. He taught me how to love God and how to love people, he deeply cared for everyone that he met. He instilled in me the importance of serving and helping others and is why I will impact millions of lives one day. I am grateful for all the quality time we spent together before he passed.

A BIG thanks to my mother **Marlene** who is a huge inspiration in my life. She is the hardest worker I know and always thinks of others before herself. I love both my parents dearly and will be forever grateful for shaping me into the person I am today.

My brother **Juan** who gave me the book Rich Dad Poor Dad by Robert Kiyosaki to read when I was 18 years old. This book gave me the idea to get into real estate and is why I purchased my first rental property at 19 years old. I probably would not be in real estate if it wasn't for him. My brother has been an amazing business partner for several different companies we own together and is a great visionary.

I want to thank my aunt **Janet** who was a real estate mogul in Miami selling condos. She was the first person to hire me and pay me to do a job. My sisters **Martha**, **Alicia**, **Anita**, and the rest of my family, thank you for always believing in me!

Thank you to my friend **Fernando Eumana**, who shared his dreams and visions with me at an early age which inspired me to go big!

Thank you to my college professor **Sunny Namkung** who would talk about owning real estate and pushed us to do something more than a 9-5 job.

Thank you to **Radovan Smolej** for keeping me accountable on finishing this book.

I want to thank my friend and driver **Daniel Duda** who always gives it his all in everything he does. Thank you to my friend and assistant **Rebecca Neighbors** who helped with editing this book.

Thank you to all the contractors, employees, team members, and vendors I have worked with. I would not be where I am today without you. Thank you to all the private money lenders who enable me to flip houses, build houses, and develop my rental portfolio.

To the men and women of our military which allows us to live in freedom, thank you for your service!

To all the clients that I helped and future clients, THANK YOU! Thank you for inviting me into your homes and letting me become a part of your family.

Stay in touch with Joshua

Send him your questions and keep up with all the
latest strategies to sell houses for top dollar via:

www.facebook.com/hometeamil/

www.linkedin.com/in/joshuainglis1/

www.instagram.com/joshuainglis/

www.joshuainglis.com

www.fifteenreasons.com

www.chicagoandburbs.com

www.ingramcontent.com/pod-product-compliance
Lightning Source LLC
Chambersburg PA
CBHW050112210326
41519CB00015BA/3938